RMW
3
22

SHAKER FURNITURE

THE CRAFTSMANSHIP
OF AN
AMERICAN COMMUNAL SECT

BY
EDWARD DEMING ANDREWS
AND
FAITH ANDREWS

PHOTOGRAPHS BY WILLIAM F. WINTER

DOVER PUBLICATIONS, INC. NEW YORK

Published in Canada by General Publishing Company, Ltd., 30 Lesmill Road, Don Mills, Toronto,
Ontario.
Published in the United Kingdom by Constable
and Company, Ltd., 10 Orange Street, London WC 2.

This Dover edition is an unabridged republica-
tion of the work originally published by the Yale
University Press in 1937. The original publication
of this work was assisted by a grant from the American Council of Learned Societies.

Standard Book Number: 486-20679-3
Library of Congress Catalog Card Number: 50-7797

Manufactured in the United States of America
Dover Publications, Inc.
180 Varick Street
New York, N. Y. 10014

CONTENTS

PLATES

(*Following page 66*)

PREFACE

THE task of gathering and examining the great mass of material essential to comprehending the philosophy of the Shaker sect and its particular expression in the domain of craftsmanship has engaged the time and attention of Mr. and Mrs. Andrews for at least fifteen years. That throughout this undertaking the methods of disciplined scholarship have been employed must be obvious to any reader of this book who is sensitive to the impact of convincing evidence carefully marshaled and clearly presented. At the same time, it is well to insist that, had the authors confined themselves to a purely objective investigation, their long labor would have achieved but barren results. The preliminary process of unearthing bare factual data entailed winning not merely the confidence but the affectionate coöperation of many middle-aged and elderly folk in still surviving Shaker communities. Adequate interpretation of the accumulated findings demanded more than knowledge, more than sympathetic insight. It involved the exercise of that extremely subtle gift of duality whereby it is possible to become spiritually merged in the extrinsic while yet preserving an unclouded intellectual point of view. In this procedure Mr. and Mrs. Andrews were notably successful. They gave their hearts to the Shakers and won a response in kind, but they never for a moment forgot their obligation to shun all sentimentality in their effort both to demonstrate the actuality of Shaker accomplishment and to reveal its underlying motives in behalf of the worldlings of today.

Their book is of singular timeliness. It comes to hand when many dwellers in the United States are concerned about prospects of change in the social structure of the nation. Under such circumstances, information is needed regarding the causes and results of whatever social experiments have hitherto been undertaken by protagonists of the perfect state. The most extensive, enduring and fruitful of such experiments was that conducted by the voluntary associations, or so-called families, of the Shakers. Although the history of that remarkable enterprise is here only incidentally treated, its actuating spirit is comprehensively analyzed by way of discovering the immaterial causes of material effects.

Another phenomenon of our current life is the emphasis placed on what is called functionalism in all the apparatus of household equipment, whether utilitarian or assumed to serve decorative ends. The dictates of functionalism insist that the design of any article shall be determined first by a study of the purpose to be fulfilled, and secondly by a consideration of the mechanical processes by which the designer's conception is to be fabricated into a reality. Functionalism eschews ornament as a superfluity and as a disingenuous attempt to conceal structure, in which, after all, resides the essence of what is often spoken of as the "new beauty."

The Shakers approached a similar ultimate from a different starting point. In their thinking, ornamentation for its own sake was a sinful indulgence. Hence all their craftsmanly products must be reduced to the lowest possible terms of form devoid of all adornment. Every article, furthermore, must be devised to meet, completely yet economically, a predetermined requirement. It must, in short, be "practical"—the word functional had not yet come into being. Sound construction and perfection of workmanship the Shakers viewed as indispensable evidence of man's willingness to labor faithfully and honestly according to God's holy ordinance. Thus without calling it by high-sounding names, they achieved a functionalism that functioned in fact without benefit of elaborate theory. Their intention was to eliminate beauty. But in spite of themselves they achieved it in forms so pure, so nakedly simple, so free from all self-consciousness, as to shame the artificial artlessness and meretricious chastity that characterize so many shrewdly reticent modern creations. So it is that Shaker furniture, no less than Shaker polity, calls for consideration from a later generation.

And yet it is by no means exclusively as a cultural critique that this volume should receive consideration. We are living in a sadly worried world. Probably not since the first fogs of the Middle Ages began to cloud an ancient civilization have so many human beings been a prey to such insistent yearnings to escape from turmoil into serenity. To very few of us is bodily retreat permitted—the quitting of the ills we have for others concealed behind the beckoning promise of lands unpioneered. Instead,

we must be content with the solace of anodynes—diversion of mind afforded by enthralling amusement or by imaginary voyages into what ret-
rospect portrays as a sweeter and less harried past. To me, at least, as
from the summit of advancing age I view the boundless domains of yester-
year, the realm of Shakerdom yields the most alluring vision of all. Time
has dimmed or quite obscured what may once have been its meaner realities. That which remains is the seeming of a life serenely fortified against
an intrusive world, of a sufficiency of all needed things and therewithal a
very real security—the fruit of happily busy hands dedicated to a pro-
pinquant God. Must not these be the attributes of that Elysium which at
the moment all mankind is so frantically striving to attain?

Though ultimately the spirit that first invoked and long sustained the
Shaker movement lost its vitality, its fragrance still abides in the now
half-deserted Shaker dwellings and in the surviving articles of Shaker
handiwork. To enter a Shaker room today is to be profoundly conscious of
this mystical emanation, at once so soothing and so strangely agitating.
That something of its essence may be conveyed, even by a pictorial tran-
script, the illustrations in this book will amply testify. They and their tex-
tual interpretation offer a doorway of brief liberation to whosoever will
but lift the latch and ponder what he finds beyond the portal. The experience should bring refreshment of soul and perhaps induce a deeper
tranquillity of mind.

HOMER EATON KEYES

SHAKER CHRONOLOGY

1706 The French Prophets open their testimony in England, near London.

1736 Ann Lee, the founder of the Shakers, born in Manchester, England.

1747 Society known as "Shakers" or "Shaking Quakers" formed by James and Jane Wardley in Bolton and Manchester. Origin of movement in the English Quaker church and the French Prophets.

1758 Ann Lee joins the Wardley society.

1772 Ann Lee, in prison, receives remarkable visions. She is acknowledged as the leader and spiritual Mother of "The Church of God."

1774 Ann Lee and a company of eight sail for America. They arrive at New York on August 6, 1774.

1776 First Shaker settlement made at Niskeyuna, or Watervliet, near Albany, New York.

1779–80 Religious revival at New Lebanon (New York) and adjacent towns. Representatives are sent to Niskeyuna, and many people are converted to the Shaker faith.

1781–83 Mother Ann Lee's mission tours through parts of Massachusetts, Connecticut and New York, build up the cause of Shakerism, and lay the foundations for a united society. A direct result of the tour was encouragement to the Believers at Harvard, Shirley and Hancock (in Massachusetts), Enfield (Connecticut) and New Lebanon (New York) to establish communities in those towns.

1784 Ann Lee dies September 8, 1784, at Niskeyuna. Elder James Whittaker succeeds her as head of the church.

1785 Father James directs that a meeting-house be built at New Lebanon. Building raised October 15, 1785.

1786 On January 29, the Believers hold their first meeting in the church in New Lebanon.

1787 Father James Whittaker dies. Succeeded by Elder Joseph Meacham, a native of Enfield, Connecticut. In September, a gathering of the society begins under Father Joseph and Mother Lucy Wright, the latter a native of Pittsfield, Massachusetts.

1788 Covenant verbally contracted at New Lebanon. "The year in which most of the members of the Church were gathered."

1790 Communities organized at Hancock, Massachusetts, and Enfield, Connecticut. (The foundation for Hancock meeting-house was laid August 30, 1786.)

1791 Meeting-house built at Niskeyuna. This community had been in process of organization since 1776.

1792 Communities organized at Canterbury, New Hampshire and Tyringham, Massachusetts. Date usually given as marking the establishment of the central church at New Lebanon in complete gospel order with a united interest.

1793 Communities organized at Enfield, New Hampshire, Shirley and Harvard, Massachusetts, and Alfred, Maine.

1794 Community organized at New Gloucester, Maine.

1795 Shaker covenant is committed to writing at New Lebanon.

1796 Father Joseph Meacham, the organizer of Shakerism on the basis of united interest, dies. Mother Lucy Wright becomes spiritual head of the church.

1805 January. John Meacham, Benjamin S. Youngs and Issachar Bates start from New Lebanon to spread the gospel of Shakerism in Ohio and Kentucky. The ultimate result of this mission was the establishment, between 1805 and 1830, of four colonies in Ohio, at Union Village (Turtle Creek), Watervliet (Beulah or Beaver Creek), Whitewater and North Union; two in Kentucky, at Pleasant Hill and South Union; and one, called West Union, at Busro, Indiana.

My Mother's wisdom is so rare
In every branch of science
That in her wisdom I can trust
And place a firm reliance.

My Mother is a carpenter
She hews the crooked stick
And she will have it strait and squair
Altho it cuts the quick.

My Mother is a Joiner wise
She builds her spacious dome
And all that trace her sacred ways
Will find a happy home.

OLD SHAKER SONG

SHAKER FURNITURE

INTRODUCTION

DURING its long existence in America, the Shaker sect, officially known as the United Society of Believers in Christ's Second Appearing, has often defined and defended its philosophy of semimonastic Christian communism. Numbers of visitors throughout this period have had the opportunity to observe the strange manner of worship, and something at least of the customs and daily routine of the followers of the mystic, Mother Ann Lee. But the literature about this native institution has been chiefly concerned with doctrinal issues and peculiarities of belief; with principles rather than practice. Little attention has been paid to the arts of the Believers: to their folk music, inspired songs and ecstatic rituals; to their religious dances and drawings; or to their fine craftsmanship in various media. Shaker furniture, in particular, merits an important place in the field of the applied arts, not alone for its perfected design but as a symbol of one of the purest of cultures.

Though the remote origins of the Shaker church lie among the Camisards of France and the English Quakers,* the twelve colonies organized in New York and New England early in the federal period were composed almost entirely of native stock, a fact which distinguishes the society of

*Certain similarities exist between the doctrines and practices of the Quakers and those of the Shakers, who were originally called "Shaking Quakers" and are often confused with the earlier sect. Both religions received inspiration from the primitive Christian church. In neither faith was there a creed, liturgy or sacrament. Fantastic manifestations of religious emotionalism characterized the early history of both sects. Both were opposed to war, the taking of oaths and litigation. Both orders avoided political activity. Instrumental music, the theater, sports and "vain amusements" of all kinds were banned. So was strong drink. Payment of just debts was enforced as a condition of membership. The status of women, in both cases, was exalted. A keen interest was taken in reforms and philanthropies, particularly in the issues of slavery and poverty. And most important of all, each society believed in the utmost practical simplicity: speech and modes of address were simple and direct; the customary symbols of grief, and all display, were discarded at funerals; dress adhered to an antique plainness; houses and furniture were unpretentious. Shakerism reflected in these various practices its early connection with the English Quaker church.

Shakers from other communistic orders in America. For most of the sects established since the founding of the Ephrata Cloister in eastern Pennsylvania over two hundred years ago, sprung from Continental, usually German, origins. The Harmonists, whose first immigrations under Father Rapp were made in 1804 and 1805; the Separatists, who settled at Zoar, Ohio, in 1817; the Community of True Inspiration, established by Christian Metz near Buffalo in 1842, and later removed to Amana, Iowa; and Dr. Keil's society set up at Bethel, Missouri, in 1844, and at Aurora, Oregon, in 1856—these were all transplanted faiths. Besides the Shakers, the only indigenous society to achieve temporal prosperity as well as a distinct, integrated culture were the Perfectionists, who settled at Oneida, New York, in 1848, a comparatively late date; and even Noyes's followers have long since departed from the national scene. The Believers, on the other hand, still pursue their unworldly ways, in five of their original eighteen communes, over a century and a half after Mother Ann first settled in the swamplands of Watervliet, New York, just prior to the Revolution.

The young men and women who were converted during the next eighteen years (1776–1794) to the gospel of Mother Ann and Father James Whittaker, her chief English supporter, were largely common people of the countryside, Puritan-Protestant stock of great vigor and idealism. Both of these leaders died soon after the movement was initiated, Ann in 1784, and James in 1787, little over a year after the first meeting-house was dedicated at New Lebanon in eastern New York. The determination and actual development of the Shaker community system, the formulation of covenantal principles and statutes, and the definitive exposition of doctrine, were the result of American leadership and influence. The customs and traditions of colonial New England and the upper Hudson River valley played an important rôle in the extension of Ann's doctrine, forming at once a foundation and point of divergence for a distinct religious order of life as well as for a specific craftsmanship.

The Shaker society was nevertheless a socio-religious phenomenon in our early national life, and its course lay in many respects as far removed from the main paths of American progress as that of other communistic sects. The Believers had little interest in the political or economic issues of the time. Marriage, private property, competitive industry and war were alike held in disfavor. The commonwealth of the spirit which was their utopia transcended nationalism and involved a faith in the eternal values of the human soul. To best combat the evils of worldliness, they followed the example of medieval orders and separated from the world of their day. And in the status of separateness, more than in any relationships to early New England traditions of thought and work, must be sought the distinction of their arts.

The virility of the Shaker movement and the definiteness of the sect's dissent from prevalent worldly customs found particular expression in a simplified, original style of furniture. The Ephratans and other German groups perpetuated foreign conventions in the applied arts; the Amanists in their household appointments appropriated decadent environmental styles; the Perfectionists expended their efforts on "rustic" furniture. The "Shaking Quakers," on the other hand, were not content with easy imitation. Though heirs of certain worthy traditions in craftsmanship, they conserved only what they considered to be the essential good in the furniture designs of their region and period. Independence of thought and action soon showed itself in the development of forms expressive of original ideas on purity, simplicity and utility.

The relationship between a way of life and a way of work invests the present study with special interest. We deal with objects finely constructed, satisfying in themselves; but also with an intensely realized faith, an unusual body of principles, a unique spiritual experience, which were embodied in customs and laws affecting the workmanship of the sect. In the prevailing animus of Shakerism lies the secret of the distinct character of the Believers' furniture, its differences from other provincial or period styles. The craft of the sect cannot be appreciated or catalogued without the introduction of this socio-religious background.

The culture and corresponding craftsmanship of the Shakers passed through three fairly distinct periods:

1. Organization into communities was a gradual process, five years elapsing from the time when Ann Lee's small colony at Niskeyuna first attracted attention (1780) to the time when the meeting-house at New Lebanon was raised, signifying the advent of a new cult. From 1787 to about 1794

converts were numerous, and all the New England and New York societies (with the exception of the colony at Sodus Bay) were founded. In the latter year the "testimony was considered closed," and attention was concentrated on consolidating the religious order and giving it meaning and form. Until the turn of the century the United Society remained detached, obscure and numerically static. During this formative stage, economic policies were formulated, characteristic industries started, dwellings and shops erected; but the production of furniture was limited. Craftsmanship was breaking away from countryside traditions, experimenting with new forms, and in the process exhibiting a somewhat unstable character.

2. By 1800 the Shaker system had become firmly established; its essential principles had become sufficiently operative to affect the secular activities of the sect; and distinct conventions in workmanship had been adopted. Until about the time of the Civil War, the culture of the Believers retained a pure and unselfconscious intensity. The members of the sect were dominated by very precise doctrines and a strict though not autocratic leadership. Reading and social intercourse were confined largely to religious channels. The church pursued its unworldly but industrious way, independent in its beliefs and practices. Conditions were favorable to the development of a true folk art; and it was to this period, when the rapid growth of the society (from 1,000 members in 1800 to a maximum of 6,000 in 1850–1860) involved a steady demand for domestic appurtenances, that the production of furniture was largely confined. So great, in fact, was the productivity of the joiners and wood turners that we can hope only to sample, pictorially and textually, the distinctive types and their main modifications.

3. By the close of the Civil War the numerical decline of Shakerism, due to various economic-religious causes, had become definitely manifest. In 1875, the recorded population was only 2,500, and by 1900 it had dwindled to a scant 1,000 again. But more important than the decrease in numbers (which removed the need for additional supplies of furniture) was the partial disintegration of the earlier pure and isolated culture. The characteristic Shaker dance rituals were slowly modified and eventually abandoned; instrumental music and more conservative songs displaced the early chants and folk spirituals; the forces of religious ardor, holding

compact the life of the sect, were wearing themselves out. The relaxation of the primary religious controls, with their attendant repressions and restraints, and the infusion of "liberal" or "broadening" ideas helped to undermine the solidarity of the order. With the influx of visitors, the employment of hired labor and the removal of restrictions on reading, contacts with the "world" became more frequent. The interiors of Shaker homes began to lose something of their severe restraint and economy: pictures appeared on the walls, secular books and newspapers on the shelves; and flowers were cultivated for their beauty and fragrance alone. The presence of all sorts of worldly gear indicated that the barriers against a sinful society had been lowered. Taste began to shift from a natural acceptance of the simple furnishings of the traditional household to a mild dissatisfaction with such simplicity and a longing for decoration and small luxuries. The furniture made in this period bears frequent evidence of the influence of Victorian style and taste, and suffers in contrast with the early forms.

Special attention is paid to the furniture made at the Church family at New Lebanon (called Mount Lebanon after 1860), which was the first society to be brought into "gospel order" and the largest eastern community. At this family, formerly known as the First Order, the first Shaker meeting-house was built and the original covenant adopted. The New Lebanon church was the "fountainhead" of Shakerism and the home of the central ministry, the supreme ecclesiastic leaders of the sect, whose delegates founded and governed other societies on the pattern of the parent colony. Even in the fields of manufacturing and craftsmanship, it was said that "The Believers at New Lebanon stood first"; and various articles made at Holy Mount* were often taken home by members of other Shaker settlements to serve as "samples" or "specimens." Though this central group thus guided the hands as well as the hearts of the various branches of the faith, each society (and each family within a society) was in truth an independent unit, conducting its own industries. The Second and North families at New Lebanon, for instance, produced furniture fully comparable in merit to that of the older group.

The artisanship of other colonies, particularly the early but still extant

* The spiritual name for the New Lebanon society.

society at Hancock (Massachusetts), has been thoroughly documented. A quantity of Alfred (Maine) furniture was obtained when that community consolidated in 1932 with the one at Sabbathday Lake (or New Glouces-ter) in the same state. This latter branch, with the two other surviving societies at Watervliet and Canterbury or East Canterbury (New Hamp-shire), is likewise adequately represented. Other eastern communes, now extinct—Harvard, Shirley and Tyringham in Massachusetts, and the Connecticut and New Hampshire Enfields—have contributed many tra-ditional pieces to the authors' collection. It has not been too late, in spite of fire and auction and neglect, to assemble and correlate hundreds of ex-amples of an essentially homogeneous workmanship.

For various reasons certain communities are excluded from considera-tion. The furniture made in the seven societies founded in Ohio, Kentucky and Indiana in the first quarter of the last century, as well as that pro-duced at Groveland (New York)—established in 1836—was marked by regional qualities which set it apart from the joinery of the older eastern colonies. An early settlement at Gorham, Maine, later (in 1819) moved to East Gloucester. Settlements made at Narcossee, Florida, and White Oak, Georgia, in the late 1890's were too short-lived to be signi-ficant.*

With certain exceptions, handicraft not directly classifiable as furniture is likewise omitted from the present study. The wood turners or me-chanics responsible for chairs, tables, beds and cases of drawers engaged in a wide variety of woodworking occupations. Countless tools, domestic utensils and accessories of all kinds exhibit an unexcelled workmanship. Baskets and boxes, coopers-ware, treen-ware, spinning wheels, reels and looms are difficult to distinguish, in inherent excellence and character, from the major appointments of the meeting-house or dwelling. Industrial devices, machines and laborsaving contrivances were made as skilfully, and in a broad sense belong in the same category, as ironing tables, tailor-ing counters, sewing and weave-stands and other industrial-use pieces. Certain types of small cabinetwork cannot consistently be neglected, but

---

* A family of colored Shakers existed for a while in Philadelphia, but was subsequently absorbed by the permanent communities. The Girlingites (English Shakers) and the Shakers of Puget Sound (Indians) had no connection with the United Society.

an extended study of all aspects of Shaker craftsmanship would complicate an already complex theme.

The authors welcome this opportunity to express their gratitude for the boundless goodwill of every Shaker family, and for the countless manifestations of friendship bearing directly on the development of their work. The inspiration and coöperation of Sisters Sadie and Emma Neale, two of the three survivors of the Church family at New Lebanon; of Eldresses Rosetta Stephens and Ella Winship of the North family; and of the late Sister Alice Smith of the Church at Hancock, are here thankfully acknowledged. To other members of these families, and to such generous leaders as Eldress Anna Case of the old Watervliet community, Sister Lillian Barlow of the Second family at New Lebanon, Eldress Fannie Estabrook of Hancock, Elder Arthur Bruce of Canterbury and Eldress Prudence Stickney of Sabbathday Lake, we are also under great obligation, for all these individuals have represented to us that intangible but real spirit of consecrated living which should illuminate all studies of this particular culture.

Nor is the record of indebtedness complete without the names of Mr. Homer Eaton Keyes, editor of the magazine *Antiques*, who was the first to recognize the importance of this native art and who inspired the continuance of our collecting and research by his wise counsel and practical encouragement; and of Mrs. Juliana Force, director of the Whitney Museum of American Art, whose recognition of the integrity and quiet elegance of Shaker craftsmanship eventuated in the present undertaking.

E. D. A.
F. A.

I
SHAKER CRAFTSMANSHIP
ITS CULTURAL BACKGROUND

THE Shaker attitude toward life and work was rooted in foundation principles so sweeping in scope as to produce a distinct philosophy and a unique American culture. These principles, which were interrelated phases of an elaborate theology based on the second coming of Christ in the person of Ann Lee, a masculine-feminine Deity, spiritual regeneration, continuous revelation and the millennium—found practical expression through the doctrines of virginal purity or celibacy, Christian communion or community of goods and separation from the world.

In its narrow original sense, purity meant freedom from carnal indulgence, but this concept (born of a special interpretation of scripture, the Puritan principle of antagonism between flesh and spirit, and doubtless on Ann's personal, tragic experiences with marriage) was expanded in the Shaker religion to include abstinence from all carnal or worldly practices. The gospel preached by Mother Ann, her brother William and James Whittaker dealt largely with primitive Christian virtues, the all-importance of freedom from evil, the absolution from sin through public confession. The first printed declaration of faith, a pamphlet written in 1790 by Joseph Meacham, successor to Ann Lee and James Whittaker as head of the church, emphasized purity and the confessional as the essential tenets of the millennial life; and the same quality and sacrament were exalted in the earliest book on Shaker doctrine, McNemar's *Kentucky Revival*, published in Cincinnati in 1807.

The doctrines of communism and separatism were a logical expansion of the principle of sinlessness. If purity was to be achieved, the Shaker leaders argued, men and women must unite in a common bond, with a common spirit of consecration—apart from the world. Celibacy and confession were therefore essential to the sacredness and perpetuity of this union: for if man "multiplies, he must divide; and an endless series of division and isolated interests must exist."* For proof, the Believers pointed to the early failure of Pythagoras and the more recent ones of Owen and Fourier "to make the community principle coalesce with the work of generation."

Though the principles of community had not been clearly formulated by the early leaders, Whittaker had anticipated the necessity of a united society with a common stock when he declared that "the time is come for you to give up yourselves, and your all, to God—Your substance, your temporal prosperity—to possess as though you possessed not." Before he died, this young but capable, dynamic leader had directed the building of the first community meeting-house and had gathered into union the scattered groups of Believers. The task of giving definite formulation to the principles of "joint-interest" and separation was then entrusted to Elder Meacham, whose genius for organization was equaled only by his great spiritual sincerity. By 1788, the Believers at New Lebanon had verbally agreed on the basic duties of a "united inheritance," which seven years later were recorded in the first covenant adopted by the Shaker sect.

This document† stated the conviction that devotion to the pure life of Christ could not be wholehearted or complete without a common faith, a common ownership of property, a common way of life. There "could be no Church in Complete order, according to the Law of Christ, without being gathered into one Joint Interest and union, that all the members might have an equal right and privilege, according to their Calling and needs, in things both Spiritual and temporal." It was also agreed that "all that should be received as members" should give what substance or property they possessed "as part of the Joint Interest of the Church . . . to be under the order and Government of the Deacons and overseers of the Temporal interest of the Church, for the use and Support of the Church, and any other use that the Gospel requires. . . ." The duty of members was not "to gather and lay up an Interest of this Worlds goods; But what we become possessed of by Honest Industry, more Than for our own support,

---

*Pelham, R. W. *A Shaker's Answer to the Oft-Repeated Question, "What Would Become of the World If All Should Become Shakers?"* Boston, 1874, pp. 20–21.

†"Order and Covenant of a Church in Gospel Order." New Lebanon, 1795. (MS. collection of authors.)

to bestow to Charritable uses, for the relief of the poor, and otherwise as the Gospel might Require."

The ideal of oneness with Christ, of the unity of the spirit, occurs continually in the early doctrinal literature of the sect, and its effect on ritual, character and workmanship cannot be overestimated. The numerous "orders" on uniformity in dress, speech, deportment and many phases of secular activity were based on the desire for a united defense against worldliness and a joint consecration to the perfect life. The covenantal belief that "we were debtors to God in relation to Each other, and all men, to improve our time and Tallents in this Life, in that manner in which we might be most useful," evoked a deep sense of mutual obligation. Spiritual union was reflected in a coöperative system of industry which conserved native ability, and in which each individual felt himself responsible for the general welfare. Pride in honorable work was kindled by the will to serve the church and to promote "the comfort and happiness of each other."

The craftsmanship of the Shakers, being a joint or community enterprise, is definitely distinguished by that fact from the products of individual effort. One result, of course, was a tendency towards uniformity. But more important was the evolution of certain standards of excellence whose widespread application was made possible by the compactness of the group and the genuineness of its ideals. Talent was stimulated by social contacts, the constant exchange and interaction of ideas and the consciousness of a united destiny. The advantages of combination were everywhere present, of special concern to us in the economies of artisanship and in the varied ingenious devices which made furniture more useful. The workmen most skilled and most keenly attuned to the spirit of Shakerism set criteria for the rest. The result was the elevation of hitherto uninspired, provincial joiners to the position of fine craftsmen, actuated by worthy traditions and a guild-like pride. The fact that the products of the cabinetmaker's art were dedicated to the use of the community as a whole, and not in any way commercialized, also invests Shaker furniture with a peculiarly impersonal quality. Possess these pieces, one hears the early elders say, as though you possessed them not.

The principle of separation, resulting as it did in a cultural isolation favorable to the development of a distinct folk life and native art, was inherent in that of communal oneness, and these two basic tenets were put into simultaneous practice. History offered a precedent in the medieval monastery, though the Shaker movement to live apart was possibly at first the result of persecution and an instinct for religious gregariousness. In the theology of the Believers, however, the ideal of separateness was traced to the Genesitic account of the fall of man. Man was corrupted by lust and could be redeemed only by complete abstinence from sexual gratification. Through the process of spiritual evolution he must be reborn into what the Shakers called the "resurrection state." Ann Lee and the early elders insisted that the "weakness of the flesh" was the cause of all worldliness: vulgarity, coarseness, dishonesty, extravagance, disorder, slothfulness, vanity and many other "vices." Because of the insidious nature of such habits, the sayings of Mother Ann included many homely injunctions bearing on the practical everyday life of the sect, of which the following are characteristic:

LABOR to make the way of God your own, let it be your inheritance, your treasure, your occupation, your daily calling.

You must not lose one moment of time, for you have none to spare.

You must . . . not allow them [the children] to be idle; for if you do they will grow up just like the world's children.

Do your work as though you had a thousand years to live, and as if you were to die tomorrow.

If you improve in one talent, God will give you more.

You must be faithful with your hands, that you may have something to give to the poor.

Put your hands to work, and your hearts to God.

Avoid equally covetousness and prodigality, be kind and charitable to the poor, and keep clear of debt.

Keep your family's clothes clean and decent; see that your house is kept clean, and your victuals prepared in good order . . .

Clean your room well; for good spirits will not live where there is dirt. There is no dirt in heaven.

. . . take good care of what you have. Provide places for your things, so that you may know where to find them at any time, day or by night . . .

You ought to dress yourself in modest apparrel [sic], as becomes the people of God, and teach your family to do likewise.

You may let the moles and bats have them [viz., gold beads, jewels, silver buckles and other ornaments]; that is, the children of this world; for they set their hearts upon such things; but the people of God do not want them.*

Separation from the "follies, vanities, contaminating principles, and wicked practices of fallen man, under the reigning influence of a depraved human nature"† was therefore an essential condition under which chastity, purity and "the resurrection of the spirit" could be obtained. There was no thought of withdrawing from "the natural creation, which is good in its order, nor from anything in it which is virtuous, commendable, or useful to his [Christ's] true followers."‡ Strictly speaking, it was from worldliness rather than the world that the Believers tried to sequester themselves: from such definable phases of corruption as personal adornment, "fanciful styles of architecture," dishonest business methods, shoddy workmanship, unnecessary elaboration of what was fine in its simplicity. Some form of cenobitic association was nevertheless unavoidable, that the Shakers might not be held "in bondage by the traditions of men." At an early date stringent orders governed all intercourse with life beyond the portals of the community.

Out of these three fundamental doctrines of Shakerism (purity, community and separation) arose a unified culture capable of distinctive patterns of expression in folkways and workmanship. One of the most important issues was the regard for simplicity, which in Shaker thought was an attribute of purity and unity. Oneness in faith was possible only on the basis of "perfect oneness of character." Of the twelve foundation pillars upholding the New-Jerusalem—faith, hope, honesty, continence, innocence, simplicity, meekness, humility, prudence, patience, thankfulness and charity—none had wider implications than "true gospel simplicity." The authors of *A Summary View of the Millennial Church* (an official statement of doctrine) defined this virtue in terms of sincerity and singleness of heart: "its thoughts, words and works are plain and simple. . . . It is

* *Testimonies of the life, character, revelations and doctrines of our ever blessed mother Ann Lee*, etc., 1816. Chapter XXX. (Counsel in Temporal Things. Industry, Cleanliness, Prudence, Economy, Giving of Alms and Charity to the Poor.)

† *A Summary View of the Millennial Church*. First edition, 1823, p. 261.

‡ *Ibid.*

without ostentation, parade or any vain show, and naturally leads to plainness in all things."*

Like cleanliness and order, simplicity was more than a fine abstraction. Through precept and example, confession and prayer and song, these virtues were translated into confirmed attitudes and habits. It was not by chance that fabrics were woven in simple patterns and dyed in limited combinations of color; that speech followed the direct Biblical injunction of "yea, yea," and "nay, nay"; that manners were humble and reserved; that costume retained certain simplicities of rural eighteenth-century style; that houses were plain, appearing in the old woodcuts of Shaker villages like geometric diagrams; that craftsmanship in iron, leather, straw or wood was so unpretentious that its art is hardly patent. Such frank, straightforward qualities proceeded from the conscious, or perhaps subconscious, practice of what amounted to a moral law. So with the related duties of innocence, meekness and humility. Conduct should be gentle and mild. "Projects of ambition" and "worldly greatness" were transgressions from the holy path. The seven "eternal" laws derived from the twelve foundation virtues—duty to God, duty to man, separation from the world, practical peace, simplicity of language, right use of property and the virgin life—helped to determine, in their varied applications, the ethos of the sect.

An elaborate disciplinary process transformed principles into practices. Precision and well-defined aims characterized educational activity and the occupations of the dwelling, shop, garden and field. In the interests of uniformity, control over the most minor aspects of behavior was attempted, as in these family orders projected early in the last century:

It is contrary to order to kneel with the left knees first.
   It is contrary to order to put the left boot or shoe on first.
   It is contrary to order to kneel with handkerchief in hand.
   It is contrary to order to put the left foot on the stairs first when ascending.†

---

*Op. cit., p. 249.

†Haskett, William J. Shakerism Unmasked, p. 178. According to Haskett, whose book was published in 1828, the "orders and gifts" comprising this constitution had never hitherto been printed. In fact, the first order of all was that it was "contrary to order for anyone to write the orders." On the title page of the Millennial Laws, or "gospel statutes and ordinances" (1845), it is stated that the orders were first "recorded" at New Lebanon, August 17, 1821, but no copy of these earlier laws is known.

Such regulations, known as "gifts" or "gifts of God," were at first periodically impressed on the members in verbal form, in the manner of the Druids. Sex-relationships were rigorously controlled, and much attention paid to the problems of cleanliness, order, humility, prudence and honesty. In 1845 these traditional rules were compiled and elaborated into manuscript order-books, known in some societies as the Millennial Laws: a secret, definitive code covering every aspect of the "resurrection life." The Laws deal with the "order, office and calling" of the ministry, the elders and deacons, the physicians and nurses; confession of sin and "opening the mind"; the "spiritual worship" of God and attendance at meetings; obligations concerning the Sabbath, Christmas, Thanksgiving and fast days;intercourse between the sexes and the language of Believers; rising and retiring, attending meals and eating; the furniture to be used in retiring-rooms; the use of books, pamphlets and writings in general; the "marking of clothes, Tools and Conveniences"; intercourse between families; travel ("going abroad") and intercourse with the world; "Literary Education, and the Schooling of Children"; and orders concerning the dead. The section on "prudence, neatness and good economy" included stringent rules to prevent loss by fire and orders on clothing, "superfluities not owned," locks and keys, dooryards and farms, beasts and "the order of the natural Creation," building, painting, varnishing and the manufacture of articles for sale.

In all these laws, precepts and principles, in the covenants of 1795 and 1801, in Meacham's declaration of faith, in McNemar's *Kentucky Revival*, in *A Summary View of the Millennial Church* and other early expositions, we find various interpretations of the doctrine of perfection, an ideal first formulated by Benjamin S. Youngs in *The Testimony of Christ's Second Appearing*, written in 1808 and sometimes known as the Shaker Bible. This interesting work expanded the millennial principle of living lives "without blemish," of conducting every act "according to godliness, sound, pure, wholesome, and free from error." The Shaker church is likened to a heavenly kingdom "because it is under the government of heaven, and is a state, habitation, or society, necessary to prepare mankind for the happiness of heaven itself." Its essential properties are unity and purity. "The Church is one in faith and practice; one in doctrine, discipline, and government; and one in the mutual and equal enjoyment of all things both spiritual and temporal."*

The perfect society, according to *The Testimony*, was a united church, not a civic body whose church embodied only the inorganic religious life of the group. The Shaker meeting-house was reserved for the forms of worship, but the dwellings and even the shops and farms were sanctified parts of the church or church society, where aspiration was transmuted into accomplishment. The idea of worship in work was at once a doctrine and a daily discipline. Labor was consecrated service, performed as in a holy place.

The monastic ideal was the pastoral or earth life, a simple economy based on agriculture and stock-raising. The patriarchal cultures of the distant past appealed to the leaders of the biblically conceived Shaker society, though the industrial conditions and demands of our early national life, the economic problems of maintaining large communities, and the mechanical skills drawn into the order with the first conversions, made it necessary to modify the idea of a utopia dependent exclusively on the soil. Many shop activities such as the sorting and packaging of garden seeds, the preparation of medicinal herbs, tanning and the drying of sweet corn and apples, were nevertheless directly related to the land; and even in those industrial branches that were partially mechanized, primitive ideals regarding the integrity of individual workmanship and a calm, unhurried devotion to task were maintained until the highly specialized methods of the "fallen world" forced the Shakers, late in the last century, to abandon most of their non-agricultural pursuits.

To such industrial and agricultural enterprises, no less than to personal behavior, did the doctrine of perfection apply. Careful organization, sound economies and many ingenious devices for facilitating and saving labor gave to the processes of every occupation a scientific character remarkable in a sect so mystic in its philosophy. The products of all Shaker shops were made for practical uses; and maximum utility, which was the aim of production, implied perfection. The capacity of any object—a machine or

---

The Testimony of Christ's Second Appearing. Second edition, 1810, p. 429. See also "A few Remarks concerning the true nature of perfection," Part VI, Chapter VII, in *A Summary View of the Millennial Church*.

tool, a building, a shop or farm product, a piece of furniture—to fulfill its appointed function with mathematical exactitude was the criterion of that object's merit. "Anything may, with strict propriety, be called perfect," the Shakers held, "which perfectly answers the purpose for which it was designed. A circle may be called a perfect circle, when it is perfectly round; an apple may be called perfect, when it is perfectly sound, having no defect in it; and so of a thousand other things."* The measuring stick, or tape measure, was to the Believer a "symbol of discipline and perfection." "I can go no farther in my work without it," writes a certain member of the order, "for positive exactness is required not only in the inches, but in the sixteenths and thirty-seconds of an inch."

In the Shaker religion the ideal was variously expressed that secular achievements should be as "free from error" as conduct, that manual labor was a type of religious ritual, that godliness should illuminate life at every point and moment. The Believers were deeply in earnest in attempting to discard the dross of worldliness, and tried, in the most devout spirit, to create products symbolical of their beliefs: products essentially useful, made "without blemish," and "redeemed" from the cheapness and vain, superfluous ornamentation of worldly manufactures. The Shaker trustees would not allow inferior or defective workmanship to go forth into the world as representative of the Millennial Church.

The application of the doctrine of perfection to creative activity, to the skilled craftsman as contrasted with the laborer or the semiskilled artisan, involves a consideration of the artistic principles affecting Shaker design. What, for instance, was the attitude of the furniture-maker, the builder, or the formulator of any fashion, toward form, color, beauty? Was the simplicity of this furniture or architecture a willed plainness, a studied avoidance of complexity and ornateness, or a naïve stylelessness? How conscious were the designers of the gulf which separates common serviceability from the sublimated utility of plain but lovely forms? Let us briefly consider two Shaker views on design, the first negative or implied and the second more positively affirmed.

The Believers associated the idea of beauty with worldly ornament, fancifulness and display. It was something extraneous, useless, superflu-

*A Summary View of the Millennial Church, p. 320.

ous, and therefore extravagant and distracting. From the early New England dissenters on the one hand, and the English Quaker faith on the other,
they had inherited a prejudice against vain show. Ostentation in dress,
pride of possession and ornamentation in architecture or handicraft were
alike detrimental to perfect oneness with Christ, diverting the spirit from
the essential realities of the "new creation." The prohibitive aspects of
Shaker "æstheticism" are well represented by that section of the Millennial Laws which concerns "Superfluities not Owned":

FANCY articles of any kind, or articles which are superfluously finished, trimmed
or ornamented, are not suitable for Believers, and may not be used, or purchased;
among which are the following; viz.

Silver pencils; silver tooth picks; gold pencils, or pens; silver spoons; silver
thimbles (but thimbles may be lined with silver); gold, or silver watches; brass
knobs, or handles of any size or kind; three-bladed knives; knife handles with
writing or picturing upon them; bone- or horn-handled knives except for pocket
knives; bone or horn spools; superfluous whips; marbled tin ware; superfluous
paper boxes of any kind; gay silk handkerchiefs; green veils; bought dark colored
cotton handkerchiefs, for sisters' use; checked handkerchiefs made by the world,
may not be bought for sisters' use, except head handkerchiefs; lace for cap bor-
ders; superfluous suspenders of any kind; writing desks may not be used by common members, only by permission of the Elders.

The following articles are also deemed improper, viz. Superfluously finished,
or flowery painted clocks, Bureaus, and looking glasses; also superfluously
painted or fancy shaped carriages, or sleighs, superfluously trimmed harness, and
many other articles too numerous to mention.

The forementioned things are at present, utterly forbidden, but if the Ministry
see fit to bring in any among the forementioned articles, which are not superfluously wrought, the order prohibiting the use of such article or articles is thereby
repealed.

Believers may not in any case, manufacture for sale, any article or articles,
which are superfluously wrought, and which would have a tendency to feed the
pride and vanity of man, or such as would not be admissible to use among themselves, on account of their superfluity.

Disapprobation of other "fancies" is expressed elsewhere in the Laws.
Thus:

ODD or fanciful styles of architecture may not be used among the Believers.

Beadings, mouldings and cornices, which are merely for fancy may not be made
by Believers.

No kinds of beasts, birds, fowls, or fishes, may be kept merely for the sake of show, or fancy.

Such contempt for useless accessories affected many phases of Shaker life and work. The prejudice against birds, for instance, is illustrated in an entry for 1831 from the *New Lebanon Ministry Sisters' Journal:*

1831: Last year where were some exertions made to gather the martin's birds round our habitations by putting up some Martin boxes; but it being too late in the season none gathered into them. Now, in the course of this week several have appeared, & seem to incline to remain. The reason for noticing this here, is because in years past, there has been a religious scruple against keeping martins, on account of their being rather an object of pride, than of usefulness. But being a report lately that they were useful in keeping off the hawks & preserving the poultry, it was considered & agreed that a trial might be made.

During the period of revival and inspiration (1837–1847), the Millennial Orders became increasingly influential, and we find in the above *Journal* such records as these:

1840. July. The four stoves that have been in the meeting room at the meeting house, have been taken out today, on account of their superfluity.

Sat. 4th. David Rowley has been employed for several days in taking out Brass knobs, and putting in their stead wood knobs or buttons (on furniture). This is because brass ones are considered superfluous, thro spiritual communication.

The substitution of social for individual ownership of property, the dedication of all goods to the common fund, and the complete absorption in the task of developing a sustaining system of agriculture and industry, tended also to undermine at the beginning one of the chief sources of personal vanity, allowing the Shakers little opportunity to indulge the "selfish" interests of leisure. Their primary mission, as expounded in an elaborate dogma of progression and cycles, was to free themselves from worldly corruptions and disease. Only after that was accomplished would there be time or "cause for Ornamentation." In the words of Elder Frederic Evans, one of the chief spokesmen of the sect, "The divine man has no right to waste money upon what you [the worldly] would call beauty, in his house or his daily life, while there are people living in misery."* Essentially the same idea is expressed by another leader at New Lebanon, Giles Avery, who felt that "the most important uses must necessarily

*Nordhoff, Charles. *The Communistic Societies of the United States,* pp. 164–165.

[first] engage attention, time and strength . . . to cut down the gigantic forests of human errors, and clear the soil of human society for the planting and culture of those goodly trees bearing the precious flowers and succeeding fruits essential to the strength and sustenance of a godly life, is primarily the duty and burden of the Christian."* "The work of drawing the lines between flesh and spirit has been so great," declares another Shaker writer,† "that there has been no time to give to any other thought but that of watching all the avenues to keep out the evils that might enter and destroy the good that has been gained." The sciences and the arts "will flourish under the patronage of those living the highest life, the Shaker life"—but only "in a future day."

Negative considerations alone, however, will not explain the character and excellence of the Believers' craftsmanship. Consistently fine work having identifiable virtues could not be the chance by-product of an escapist philosophy, of a religion whose emphasis was solely on the uprooting of evil. To appreciate the merit of the furniture made by the Believers, attention must ultimately be shifted to the expansive forces in their culture, to their life work in its total aspect.

This broader point of view enables us to see an unspoiled culture, an "unhelped people," with a native instinct for good workmanship, and a regard for form and design which was given direction and meaning by certain moral-scientific-inspirational values of unusual import. The early craftsmen left scant record of their creed,‡ but at a later date, in the writ-

---

The Shaker, August, 1876, Vol. VI, No. 8, p. 58.

†Mace, Aurelia G. *The Aletheia: Spirit of Truth*, p. 74.

‡One Shaker craftsman, however, the clockmaker Benjamin Youngs, as early as 1805 gave evidence of the artist-consciousness when he wrote that "in building a house, or constructing any machine, each part naturally lies in apparent confusion till the artist brings them together, and puts each one in its proper place; then the beauty of the machinery and the wisdom of the artist are apparent." (Brown, Thomas. *An Account of the People called Shakers*, 1812, pp. 293–294.)

The religious conception of creative activity was finely phrased in Youngs's comparison of the Shaker church to the temple of Solomon:

"God is the great artist and master-builder, the gospel is the means, the ministration are his labourers, and instruments under his direction, and we must labour in union with them to cast away all rubbish out of, and from around the building; and to labour to bring everything, both outward and inward, more and more into order."

ings of numbers of Believers, declarations appear which reveal what must always have been, in the society, the tests of worthy achievement. Thus:

REGULARITY is beautiful.

There is great beauty in harmony.

Order is the creation of beauty. It is heaven's first law, and the protection of souls.

Love of Beauty has a wider field of action in association with Moral Force.

Beauty rests on utility.

All beauty that has not a foundation in use, soon grows distasteful, and needs continual replacement with something new.

That which has in itself the highest use possesses the greatest beauty.

Regularity, harmony, order. The whole history of Shakerism gives evidence that these were cardinal principles. Document after document asserts the necessity of such virtues in a community modeled on the vision of the heavenly kingdom. Such values undeniably affected the work of the furniture artisan, guiding his search for chaste design and unity of form.

The moral obligation to do work which was worthy of a sacred cause, kindled the desire to raise one of the essentials of fine craftsmanship, utility, to such a level of perfection that Shaker products assume a formalized character not possessed by ordinary utilitarian objects. Was this urge to do more than common necessity demanded, and more than average ability could attain, an impulse compensating for those religious restrictions which confined expression to the applied arts, to simple forms and tempered colors? Or was it the result of the true craftsman's attitude toward the task at hand, whether great or small? Surely, the perfecting of utility and the designing of forms pure and refined were possible only by the expenditure of a high quality of skill—technical ability which, to use Conrad's words, embraced "honesty and grace and rule in an elevated and clear sentiment, not altogether utilitarian, which may be called the honor of labor." In the last analysis, efficiency of this character was more than flawlessness: "something beyond—a higher point, a subtle and unmistakable touch of love and pride beyond mere skill; almost an inspiration which gives to all work that finish which is almost art—which *is* art."*

The responsiveness of the Shaker "mechanic" to the ethical influences

*Conrad, Joseph. *The Mirror of the Sea*, New York, 1906, p. 37.

about him, his spiritual identification with the sheerly simple character of his work, and his insistence that such work should not ignore or defy in any way "its own reason for being," placed him in fact on the plane of the artist, and his various "utilitarian" achievements are as much the expression of the Shaker soul as are the paintings or sculptures of other times and other cultures. His maxims that beauty rests upon utility, and that love of beauty must have a basis in morality, illustrate what the Shakers have often asserted about their faith, that it combined "science, religion and inspiration," and that these concepts, " 'truly so called,' are one and the same." How close to their sympathies would have been the assertion of the English craftsman, William Morris, that "in the artist, and therefore in his art, a certain moral quality was before all things essential"; his rule to "have nothing in your houses that you do not know to be useful, or believe to be beautiful"; or his belief that by an "accumulation of useless things not only are beautiful things kept out, but the very sense of beauty is perpetually dulled and ground away!"*

The definite sense and mastery of design which characterize the furniture of the sect were the result, no doubt, of a number of interesting influences: it matters little whether emphasis is placed on the negative or positive, or to what extent merit is traceable to conscious or æsthetic motives. It does matter that the Believers were dedicated to "primitive rectitude" in conduct and to "rightness" in the work of the hands. The peculiar correspondence between Shaker culture and Shaker artisanship should be seen as the result of the penetration of the spirit into all secular activity.

Current in the United Society was the proverb: "Every force evolves a form."

*Mackail, J. W. *The Life of William Morris*, London, 1899, Vol. II, pp. 63–64.

II
SHAKER FURNITURE
ITS ESSENTIAL CHARACTER

IT is clear that everything was subordinate to religion. All the values in Shaker culture proceeded from primitive scriptural dogmas revivified by the peculiar personalities and interpretations of Ann Lee and the early elders; from the principles of celibacy, communism, separatism and the glorification of manual labor; from the belief in order and cleanliness, simplicity and economy; from the "twelve Christian virtues" and "seven moral principles"; from the doctrine of utilitarianism; from the philosophy of the superfluous; and from the Christian ideal of charity and the golden rule. A stream of revelation, extending from the apocalypse of St. John to the visions of the French Prophets, from the inspirations of Ann Lee to the "gifts of God" and the Holy Laws of Zion,* fortified such dogmas and clothed them with divine authority. Little wonder that that picturesque mid-century wanderer and student of American social experiments, A. J. Macdonald, recorded in his notebook the belief of the Shakers at Niskeyuna that their furniture was originally designed in heaven and that the patterns had been transmitted to them by angels.†

The strictly mundane origins of Shaker stylism in furniture, however, lie in the craft traditions of colonial New York and New England. The joiners welcomed into the early church were provincial workers following conventions which had been subjected to little change for over a century. Similarly, the furniture brought into the embryonic societies and consecrated to the "joint interest" consisted largely of the unpretentious, humble possessions of farmers, mechanics and small tradesmen—the common

---

*"The Holy Laws of Zion" (MS.) were written by Philemon Stewart, an inspired instrument at New Lebanon, in 1840. They formed one of the chief immediate sources of the Millennial Laws.

†Noyes, John Humphrey. *History of American Socialisms*, pp. 602–603. Much of Noyes's material for this volume came from the data collected by Macdonald.

people of the day. Though a scattered few of the first converts had some professional standing and means, the first houses occupied by the Shakers contained on the whole an insignificant and meager assortment of slat-back chairs, cottage beds, candlestands, plain and often crude tables, New England chests and cases of drawers, and a miscellany of tools, kitchen utensils, farm implements and accessories. A few Windsors, banister-back and Dutch-style chairs found their way into the communities, as well as an occasional stretcher table, inlaid chest of drawers or highboy. Any piece of furniture was useful, and nothing was at first rejected because of its ornate appearance.

The communal dwellings, meeting-houses and shops erected within five years after the sect was organized could not, however, be adequately equipped with such a paucity of material. The first "great House" at New Lebanon was raised as early as August 27, 1788, and occupied by Christmas. Another home, called the "East House," was completed on April 21, 1791, a house for the aged members in the following June, and one for the "youths" on August 21, 1792. In this year the Church or First Order numbered 214 Believers, 109 males and 105 females, whose average age was only twenty-four. The membership of all branches of the United Society totaled a thousand converts—relatively poor people, who could not contribute much to the common fund. Unable, had they wished, to purchase necessary furnishings, the early Shakers preferred to supply their own needs as far as possible. Socio-religious ideals found immediate expression in a vigorous industrial program. A chair factory, tannery, blacksmith shop and fulling mill were in operation at New Lebanon by 1789. The same year a brethren's brick shop was erected, and soon the Believers of this colony were producing coopers-ware, felt hats, whips and whip-lashes, hoes, harness, shoes, wrought nails, shoe and stock buckles and other useful articles. The building of a "spin-shop" in 1791 stimulated the manufacture of cloth and clothing. The last decade of the eighteenth century witnessed the origin of the important garden seed and broom industries, and an increased activity in the making of furniture and household and shop appurtenances of every kind.

Immersed as the Shakers were in the spirit and obligations of the new religion, subject to the exacting standards of conscience, and confronted

by the unprecedented conditions of community organization, the craftsmen of this busy formative period were nevertheless not content to repro-
duce existent designs in furniture. Such pieces as the highboy and lowboy,
the canopy-bed, various types of tables, and chairs in the banister-back,
splat-back, Windsor or cabriole-leg style were rejected not only because
they were more difficult to make than simpler types, but because the
Shakers, under the recent influence of Ann Lee's teaching, desired no
commerce with pretense or worldliness. More important still was their
dissatisfaction with the plainer forms of contemporary candlestands,
trestle and stretcher-base tables, linen chests, low-post beds and colonial
slat-back chairs. The Shaker cabinetmakers sought to free their workmanship at the outset from all semblance of ornament. Just as they had committed themselves to the cardinal virtues, so they placed emphasis on the
cardinal principles rather than the minor, superficial flourishes of craftsmanship.

The eventual result of this penetration of religion into the workshop,
as we have noted, was the discarding of all values in design which attach
to surface decoration in favor of the values inherent in form, in the har-
monious relationship of parts and the perfected unity of the whole. Under
such conditions, if the design was well conceived, an effect of rare charm
was achieved. But no accessories, carvings, extravagant turnings, veneer-
ings or inlays were present to distract the eye from whatever faults may
have corrupted the original plans.

The ideal of purity, broadly conceived as it was, furnished sufficient
justification for such a theory of workmanship. Elder Giles Avery definitely specified as an act of "deception," even of "adultery," the practice
by worldly cabinetmakers of "dressing . . . furniture of pine or white
wood with the veneering of bay wood, mahogany or rose wood." A natural frankness characterized the finished Shaker product, which was enhanced by the light stains and varnishes which supplanted at an early period
the heavier stains or paints. One's primary impression, on seeing an
assemblage of Shaker pieces, is that of brightness and lightness more expressive of serene happiness than somber monasticism. Is not this evidence of the quiet joy of the Shaker life, a joy disclosed in the ecstatic rituals of worship, and restrained but not suppressed in the daily experience

of the order? Life was indeed subject to constant discipline, but those who had caught the inspiration pursued their course with an inner exuberance of spirit. The simple routinized existence, though abnormal in its repression of sex, was otherwise close to elemental forces, and instinctively averse to sophistication. The love of nature, recorded in many an early Shaker writing,* was in accord with, if it does not partially explain, the appreciation of what may be termed a "natural" craftsmanship: work which left the beauty of the wood itself unspoiled and unconcealed.

An effect of subdued elegance, even of delicacy, was achieved, especially in chairs, small tables, stands, desks and sewing cabinets, by restraint in the preparation of materials. In the largest chairs, the posts may measure only a trifle over an inch in diameter. The tops of candlestands or sewing stands, the legs of tripod stands and the rockers of chairs may be reduced to half an inch in thickness. Such diminution in the elements of a design was not the result of a desire to conserve material, of which there was an abundance—as witness the heavy stock in much case-furniture—but to an obvious instinct for style. As their products were seldom intended for a "sinful" world, the joiners were not forced to anticipate careless handling and misuse.

Though the quality of furniture was thus quietly dignified and uncomplicated, its function in the service of a complex community organization was at once precise and differentiated. The Shaker economic system symbolized the historic transference of occupations from the home to the shop or small factory; and new industries were conducted on a scale requiring laborsaving devices and progressive methods. The versatility of the

---

*Read, for example, Elkins (pp. 44–48, 78, 80), Harris (pp. 23–24), Baker (p. 15), Pomeroy (p. 8), Howells (pp. 108–109), etc. See Bibliography. Life in the "great days" of the Shakers was not unduly ascetic, even though it was an outgrowth of Puritanism. Religion was expression more than repression.

Nor were the Believers without certain physical comforts. Old account books reveal importations of "Shere," Malaga, port and sweet wine, New England rum, "Brande," spirits and gin. The early Shakers saw no fault in distilling spirits and making wines themselves, though intoxicating drink was portioned out with great care. In the years before the Anti-Tobacco testimony, the fragrant weed was used by brethren and sisters alike; and many a Shaker peddler returned with tobacco and "Snuf" from the market towns.

Shaker workmen is well illustrated by the countless tools invented for unprecedented techniques.

The furnishing of dwellings, housing "families" of thirty to over a hundred sisters and brethren, also presented distinct problems. Domestic activities were conducted on a coöperative basis, and the furniture and industrial equipment of the home had to be amply scaled and intimately accommodated to the communal order of housekeeping. This adaptation to the needs of groups rather than individuals gives a typical character to a great deal of Shaker furniture. Sewing stands were equipped with drawers which could slide from either side as two sisters worked on a project together. Desks were made with double tablets, sets of drawers and shelves. Two or more ironers could work at one time on the long laundry tables. Cases of drawers in the retiring-rooms conformed to the requirements of a number of occupants. Large cupboards and long benches and dining tables were characteristic, not exceptional pieces. Quantity production remained comparatively free, however, of that stereotyped design and finish which makes the institutional equipment of the machine age so ugly.

Certain elements of cabinet design, which were the logical expression of ideas on utility or convenience, refinement or simplicity, further serve to give a definitive style to Shaker furniture. Mention may here be made of the rod-shaped or subtly tapered turnings of stand- and table-legs, with foot or terminal shaping entirely omitted; the neatly turned pegs which served as drawer pulls; the significant absence of escutcheons and brasses; the profiled patterns of stand-legs and chair-rockers; the sharply angled bracketing of the feet on counters, cases and chests; the large wooden casters or rollers on beds; the ball-and-socket device on the back posts of early side chairs; the peculiar underbracing of benches and trestle tables; the narrowness of cupboard doors, and their control by ingenious wrought-iron catches; the drop-leaf commonly attached to the back of tailoring counters, side tables or sewing cabinets; the comparative lowness of chairs, tables and stands; the frequent addition of small, unenclosed, extra drawers on stands or long tables; exposed dovetailing and a frequent omission of moldings; the characteristic and uniform use of reds, yellows and greens, and of light varnishes and oil stains; the checkerboard colored listings used on the seats of the later-type chairs.

The imaginative faculty, seeking to clothe utility in ever-new forms, often evolved original units such as the sewing desks, so called, the designs of which vary greatly in different societies, and even within a given community. Combination pieces were also common: benches enlarged to serve as tables, stands or desks; table-counters and table-desks; wood-boxes equipped with towel racks or joined with washstands; and so on. Long low tables, each having a tier of cupboards with paneled doors below, served in the old Enfield (New Hampshire) kitchens both as convenient receptacles for pans and pots, and as movable worktables. The high and low swivel-stools, the pegboards which line the walls of almost every Shaker room, and the mirrors and wall-clocks suspended from these pegs, were also unique productions. Towel racks and wall-sconces, oval and writing-boxes, step-stools and many other items of small cabinet-work exhibit characteristics of a specific style. The regard for perfected work, stamped as it is on every product great and small, further distinguishes the Shaker joiners' craft. In the furniture of the shop—cobblers' and carpenters' benches, for instance—we find the same faithful attention to detail as was applied to the most important pieces in the dwelling-house.

It is not strange that in each Shaker society in the East, comparable patterns of furniture should be encountered. Even in the Ohio and Kentucky communities we find the typical, simplified trestle table, the severely designed chest and a close relative of the eastern chair. The units of the commonwealth of Believers were closely federated, in secular as well as religious practice: there was "an almost perfect uniformity among them, of dress, language, manners, forms of worship, government, etc."* The family or society covenants of every community were modeled on the original document of the New Lebanon church, which furnished also the pattern of internal organization. The central ministry at this place exercised a general supervision and control over all the societies, and constant intervisitation and correspondence were carried on between the leading "influence" here and the "leads" of other communes or bishoprics.† The

---

*Lamson, David R. *Two Years' Experience among the Shakers*, p. 18.

†Two or more Shaker societies were united to form bishoprics, which were governed by ministries, each composed of two elders and two eldresses appointed by the central ministry at New Lebanon.

all-importance of unity we have noted: the Millennial Laws and the circulars issued by the ministry re-enforced the principle of uniformity and gave specific details on such matters as the furnishing of rooms and the finishing and care of furniture.*

Other influences tending toward the development of a uniform style of craftsmanship may thus be summarized:

1. The assignment of artisans and cabinetmakers from one society or family to another to coöperate on industrial and constructional enterprises.†

2. The similar shop equipment required by similar occupations.

3. The concentration of a certain industry in a given family or society from which the product was distributed to other branches of the organization. New Lebanon was thus the center of the Shaker chair business.

4. Principles of design, in chairs as in other types of furniture, worked out in the parent colony of New Lebanon, undoubtedly influenced style in other communities.‡

*Authorized Rules of the Shaker Community, p. 16. Uniformity in all things was considered by the lead an essential of communal unity. The reasons given by Elder Giles Avery, a member of the central ministry, in his "Circular concerning the dress of Believers" (c. 1866), are characteristic: " There are very strong reasons in favor of uniformity, both in style, or pattern of dress, and color and quality of dress fabrics; each one, and all of these subjects, effects, materially the welfare and prosperity of Believers, both spiritually, socially and financially. Spiritually, because, uniformity in style, or pattern in dress, between members, contributes to peace and union in spirit, in as much as the ends of justice are answered, and righteousness and justice are necessary companions."

†Shaker meeting-houses, family dwellings, large barns, etc. were often erected by "mechanics" from more than one community, contributions toward the cost being sent in from all the societies. Thus, when the second church at Watervliet was built in 1848, New Lebanon sent such master craftsmen as Amos Stewart, George Wickersham, Isaac Youngs, Amos Smith, James Wilson and James Bishop to assist in the work. The building was planned by Freegift Wells of the Watervliet colony, who also assisted Wilson in the masonry. The roofing was done by Wilson and Smith, the inside finishing by Stewart and Wickersham, and the clapboards and blinds by Wickersham and Loren Wicks of Watervliet.

‡On her frequent visits to New Lebanon, for example, Mother Hannah Goodrich of the first ministry at Canterbury and Enfield (New Hampshire) would often "obtain some article to take home as a model of religious care as exercised by the Brethren and Sisters of the Parent Society." An excerpt from the Church journal at Canterbury reads: "We often received specimens of the various kinds of manufacture as samples, made in the most substantial and perfect manner, such as leather, sieves, clothing, boots and shoes, pails, small oval boxes, hoes, nails and other articles." (Shaker Manifesto, August, 1882, Vol. XII, No. 8, p. 173.)

5. The "wholesale" manufacture of furniture parts in one society for shipment to and subsequent assembling in other communities.*

Yet exact uniformity could not be achieved. Regional influences of a subtle character tended to differentiate the craftsmanship of communities and even the work of the families in a given society. Each family had its own covenant. The Millennial Laws were subject to varied interpretations and degrees of enforcement by different ministries or family elders; in some groups, indeed, such orders may never have been actually recorded. The personality of the leadership, vicissitudes in the life of a communal organization, the economic independence of the family unit and differences in local traditions, added to the difficulty of attaining absolute sameness in secular matters: in dress, occupation, revenue or style of furniture.

Although variety existed "in uniformity," Shaker cabinetwork was nevertheless a homogeneous craftsmanship, with the specialized character arising from common standards and common needs. Trestle tables may vary in length and height, in the form of the posts and in the shaping of the feet, yet each example conforms to a hypothetical type. The drawers and cupboards ot case-furniture may be arranged in many patterns, but certain details of construction, as well as the general aspect of a given example, will usually bespeak its provenance. Chair finials and arms have subtle variations of form not definite enough to serve as a key to community origin (as some have asserted), nor so extreme as to lead to erroneous attribution. Not even the intermittent "improvements" in late period chairs and other furniture can wholly obscure the "unmistakable Shaker look"—emphasized when such pieces are seen in their historic setting.

The Believers' craftsmanship retained its distinctive purity during a long period when art and fashion in America, subject to foreign dictation and the whims of a rapidly expanding materialistic culture, deteriorated

*An instance of such pre-factory age specialization is found in a letter written on November 30, 1829, from Port Bay (Sodus Bay or Sodus Point, New York) by John Lockwood, a Shaker cabinetmaker, informing Deacon Stephen Munson of the New Lebanon church that Lockwood was sending on "some Cherry bords nine in number amounting to one hundred feet, also 2 bunches of table leges 68 in number."

or wavered in quality. From this world of change the sectarian furniture shops were completely isolated. Chairs marketed throughout the whole of the last century adhered to the early style. For seventy years or more after the communities were founded, all classes of joinery resisted the effect of the vagaries in worldly taste. The shop was the immediate servant, a projection of the home, its pervading spirit in harmony with the prevailing tenets of the order. The status of the home, moreover, as that of a permanently fixed institution from which the Shakers never expected to depart, also accounts in no small measure for the scientific adaptability of their furniture, the painstaking thoroughness with which it was executed and its constant character.

III

THE CRAFTSMEN OF THE SECT

IN the examination of the principles and practices which characterized the competent art of the Believers, emphasis has been placed on the religio-communistic quality of Shakerism. The communal nature of all industrial or craft enterprise resulted in a furniture largely devoid of those marks of individuality which make it possible to distinguish the work of one craftsman from that of another. It is helpful, nevertheless, to consider the human, personal aspects of this trade, not only to appreciate such matters as the selection and training of artisans, their equipment and working conditions, but to call attention to that spirit of independence, particularly in the more creative phases of production, which is not normally associated with a communistic economy.

The Shaker joiner was a free and self-reliant craftsman. Usually he worked by himself, or with an apprentice or two; and though often interrupted by various unrelated duties, he was responsible for each project's skilful and early completion. Profit considerations did not condition the work of the wood turners' shop, and the principles of division of labor and scientific coöperation on which most Shaker industries depended for their success here played a minor rôle. Cabinetmaking was thus a less standardized occupation, and one allowing for the expression of some personality. To evoke the actual setting in which the industry of making furniture was carried on, to recall something of the attitude of the wood turner toward his work, even to register the names of the humble but inspired monastic laborers, will therefore clarify the character of this particular school of craftsmanship.

The earliest furniture was produced by individuals whose attitude toward life, in consequence of their absorption in Shakerism, had undergone a complete change. But workmanship was not at first uniform in character: many craftsmen continued to labor in their own homes or shops, or in families partially organized under the leadership of prominent Believers. The testimony against extravagance and "superfluity" worked itself out in a multitude of forms, those patterns surviving which accorded most truly with the needs and spirit of the new order. With the adoption of the covenant, the temporal organization of the church, and the construction of shops, the furniture industry assumed a greater degree of consolidation, and rapidly acquired traditions which were adopted by novitiates to the order.

Continuity in the quality and design of furniture was further preserved by an informal apprenticeship system. When boys were committed to the elders or trustees of a Shaker family by their parents or guardians, the legal indentures* provided that these minors should be taught in "such manual occupations or branch of business as shall be found best adapted or most suitable to their genius and capacity." While still in the Children's Order, boys with an interest in mechanical pursuits were thus allowed to spend some time in the brethren's shops, where they became acquainted with the use of tools and imitatively constructed simple objects. Other boys were apprenticed to tailors, hatters, broom-makers, cobblers, gardeners or seedsmen. All attended the three months' winter session of school, and were responsible for miscellaneous chores: from the first, training was directed to proficiency in more than one occupation. The Shakers believed in rotation of labor and variety of industry, for such was "a source of pleasure."

The principle of diversity of occupation, with the emphasis on specific training along certain lines, is illustrated by the report of an early Canterbury caretaker on the winter's work, mornings and evenings, of one of his charges:

ONE of the pupils, a youth of fourteen years of age, made three wood boxes; one of a large size, the sides being fastened together with joists and spikes; the others designed for the furnishing of dwelling rooms, were made nice, being fitted together in the manner of a reversed wedge, or (in carpenters' language) dovetailed: bottomed two chairs with flag; one with woven strands; covered eight or ten with leather; made four pairs leather mittens; seven pairs gloves; twenty axe helves; and split and drew the wood for the family laundry.†

*Andrews, Edward D. *The Community Industries of the Shakers*, pp. 31, 268.
†Elkins, Hervey. *Fifteen Years in the Senior Order of Shakers*, p. 79.

If the Children's Order were large enough, the caretaker conducted the boys into the "art and mystery" of various vocations in their own shops. In cases where there were only a few children, guardians were appointed. Thus, when Giles Avery entered the New Lebanon Office family in 1821, as the only boy in that order he was placed under the tutelage of Benjamin Lyon, a skilled artisan from whom the youth probably received his first lessons in mechanical technique.* Amos Stewart was similarly indentured to Nathan Kendal of the Church in February, 1811, when he was but nine years old. Here he came under the spiritual influence of Mother Lucy Wright, Rufus and Ebenezer Bishop, Ruth Landon, John Farrington and others; here he associated with such temporal leaders as Stephen Munson, Israel and Amos Hammond, David Meacham and Edward Fowler; and here he may have worked in the early chair shop of Asa Tallcott, in the joiners' shop of Gideon Turner or Amos Bishop, in the machine shops of Benjamin Bruce or Benjamin Lyon, or in the coopers' shop of Henry Markham. In March, 1823, Stewart was admitted into full "covenant relationship" in the Church, and for nearly sixty years served the society as elder and minister. Throughout this period, however, he continued his industrial labors, making some of the finest and most characteristic cupboards and cases of drawers produced at the parent colony.

In such a self-sufficient order as that of the Shakers, with its complex occupational requirements, the skill of the more talented individuals was often widely distributed. Isaac Youngs of New Lebanon was not only a clocksmith, but a cabinetmaker, tailor, farmer, mason, blacksmith and teacher. In addition to cabinetwork, wagon-making and the manufacture of wooden dippers, the aforementioned Giles Avery engaged in building repair, stonemasonry, plumbing, carpentry and plastering. Elder Hervey L. Eads of South Union, Kentucky, was a shoemaker, teamster, seed grower, tailor, bookbinder, wool carder, spinner, tin and sheet-iron worker, dentist, printer and hatter—as well as an author and a bishop. Richard McNemar, another western leader, was a religious scholar and hymnologist, a preacher, journalist, printer and editor; but he worked also at making chairs, weaving cloth, binding books, and manufacturing spinning wheels and reels. These cases were not exceptional.

*Concerning Benjamin Lyon, see Andrews, *op. cit.*, pp. 116–118.

In such a flexible system, the carpenters, joiners or wood turners whose main employment was furniture-making, might at various periods be shifted to building construction, coopering, shingle-making, turning handles or even to work in the gardens, fields or mills. The patternmakers who formulated the designs for industrial devices and machines probably coöperated in their actual construction, enlisting the services of the mechanic, the blacksmith and the joiner. Such shifting from one occupation to another was usually an informal procedure supervised by the family deacons or trustees; but on rare occasions, if a member took too vain a pride in his work, permanent transference to another branch of industry was ordered by the elders or ministry. None were required, however, "to labor beyond their strength and ability." The ministry, elders and trustees joined the commonest members in the humblest labors. All were equal in spirit, and all contributed alike to the welfare of the order.

The system of rotation and change in occupation affected the quality of workmanship in several ways. Since no one, with the possible exception of the chair-maker, confined his attention to a single pursuit, it was easier to follow the established tradition of simple design than to experiment with more difficult forms. The more skilful joiners, in particular, were called upon to do such a multitude of jobs that the most direct and economical method of finishing a given piece of furniture was also the most practical one. Variety in industry, on the other hand, militated against stereotyped performance: the joiner did not make one case of drawers or bed after another, but approached each project freshly from some other calling. Production was always for use; work was incessant but seldom hurried. Emergencies rarely existed and he could choose his own time to finish the work at hand. The craftsman labored neither for master nor market demand, but for a community which he believed would be timeless. Pursuing the millennial ideal of mutual helpfulness, woodworkers also went from house to house, from family to family, and often from one society to another. They borrowed freely what was best in each community, and thus helped to preserve the highest standards of craftsmanship.

The joiners' shop was often open at five o'clock in the morning, or in the winter, a half hour later. Sundry chores were performed before the six or half-past six breakfast; fires were started in the small cast-iron stoves and "stuff" prepared for the day's work. After the morning meal, the "mechanics" repaired to their varied occupations. A request from the deacon or elder of the family, or from the deaconess or eldress, might require the construction of a case of drawers, a particular kind of counter, or a long table for use in a kitchen or herb-shop. If the stock were not on hand, the cabinetworker would often go to the sawmill himself. He planned the piece in his mind's eye, familiar with types already made for similar purposes: for rarely, it seems, was the design executed on paper beforehand. His labor was straightforward: fine tools and machine and foot-lathes were present; stains, oils, varnishes and paints were part of the shop's equipment. He might, however, be interrupted before the twelve o'clock dinner by demands from other shops and trades: a mechanic might be needed for repairs in the washhouse; an unexpected problem might await solution in the weave-shop; the seedsmen might be shorthanded in boxing seeds for immediate delivery; or an order for broom handles might claim priority. In such cases the cupboard, counter or table had to wait until the emergency was over. The wood turner took up his complex routine soon after the frugal noonday repast, and worked till the bell on the roof of the dwelling sounded the five-minute warning for supper at six o'clock. Often he returned afterwards to put the shop in order, to see that fires were extinguished, sometimes to work by the fading daylight or the gleam of candles.

Production was accelerated when a new dwelling, with its manifold requirements for fixed and movable furniture, was nearing completion. At such times the available skill of an entire family or society was needed to build the scores of cases, tables, cabinets, beds and other furnishings required. Only then did the wood-turning shops assume the appearance of a scale-production establishment. Repetition of motif prevailed: the plans for one retiring-room were like those for another. And there was division of labor: some worked with the mortising machine, turning lathe or planer, while others confined their attention to such operations as dovetailing, applying knobs to drawers and finishing. But never did the amount of labor on hand reduce the rules of simplicity to the point of crudeness, vitiate activity with carelessness, or obscure the vision of inspired and unblemished workmanship.

The following extracts from the journal of Henry DeWitt, a mechanic and joiner at New Lebanon, illustrate the varied day-by-day routine of the typical Shaker artisan. A native of Canada, DeWitt entered the society at Watervliet in 1813, moving the same year to the parent community. Employed at cutting and heading nails until 1823, he was then transferred to the "shoemaking business." In November, 1827, he started to work with one Levi Chauncey at the wheel and reel-wright business. For variety he wove baskets. The journal continues:

DEC. 1827 Levi & I began to make a lot of great spinning wheels.

　Fri. 21 I made a couple of drawers to put under the vise bench.

　Mond. 24 We began to make a small case of drawers with a cupboard at the top of it.

　Tues. 25 This day we celebrate in memory of our blessed Lord and Saviour.

　Sat. 29 We finished our case of drawers all but staining.

　Jan. 1828 Tues. Levi & I began to mend old baskets & chairs.

　Sat. 12 Mended 18 baskets & 3 chairs.

　Tues. 15 I made a couple of books

　Fri. 18 I mended 24 chair bottoms

　Mond. 21 I fixed a saw plate in a bow & cut new teeth & filed it.

　Jan. 31 "My work is so often changed; it is hard to give a true statement of it."

> Sometimes a fixing spinning wheels,
> At other times to work at reels;—
> If I should mention all I do,
> My time and paper would be few.

Feb. 1828 Fri. 1 cut a walnut tree for basket bails & rims

　4 turned 52 reel legs

　5 I polished & straightened spindles.

　10 I turned about 40 wheels for clock reels.

　12 I worked sawing out the cogs to the reel wheels.

　13 About 4 I came in the shop; made a box dufftaled it read for the cover & bottom

　14 I finished the said box. It was for Moses M. to put pipe stems in.

　Oct. 1828 Mond. 20 I began to make a new constructed weavers scarn; having short pegs at the bottom; and short pins at the top to let in about 2 inches.

　Tues. 21 I nearly finished my scarns.

The next few years find DeWitt engaged in countless jobs: turning bristle-brush handles, banisters, wheel-spokes, wheel-standards, etc.;

"figuring off" reels; whitewashing buildings; laying stone walks; making drains; "cutting onion seeds"; plowing, planting and haying. The journal continues:

July 1832 In the morning I commenced turning closepins for the great house. I turned pins all this week excepting Thirsday I mended shoes. I turned 604 pins this week.

Sept. 1832 I turned 71 Whurs for curtain strings to run on. I made a sink for the sisters in the lower room at the east house.

March 1833. I commenced a new kind of business. It was making little spools for to weave tape with. Made the barrels of tin & heads of pewter.

I have been nearly all the week making said spools. Made 160. I have been turning drawer buttons for 2 days past—turned 200

November 1833 I let John Shaw have 2 bushels of pegs at 2$ per bushel.

March 1834 The two past weeks; after doing my days work at making cloth shoes; I have employed myself at making a loom; or began to make one. It is to replace the loom that was bought, it proved nothing at all. In the morning I commenced working on my loom and expect to continue. I have been working at said loom the week past. . . . I finished said loom. It was stain'd yesterday. Eleanor P. & Jane B. stain'd it.

I have been about 4 weeks making this spring shuttle loom. I took my new loom over to the spinshop and set it up for weaving. beamed on about 30 yds of course linen. Betsy Crossman wove some & it went well.

May 1834 I made me a try-square one foot long. I took it from the rough both the tongue and the wood—the tongue was taken out of a piece of saw plate—my wood was lingumvite—blued the tongue after I polished it—put it together and straightened it fit for use.

In June, 1834, DeWitt took over another responsibility: the making of journals and "tune" books. His experience with shoemaking accounts for his ready ability to bind these books in leather, sometimes tooled. Apparently he had some pride in this workmanship, for he affixed a small blue label to his product: "Bound by Henry DeWitt. New-Lebanon."

March 1835 In the A.M. I assist Peter Long about crimping boots & cutting them out. The rest part of the day I worked at books. I put the covers on 5 books besides some other business. In the A.M. I level my work bench. In the P.M. I begin to get out some timber for bobins. I have been getting my timber ready for turning bobins. builded 3 books, & cut out 3 pairs shoes. I make a beginning to buz out a lot of wood heels. I got out willow enough for 19 more spools. I turned out 52 warping spools by 4 oclock.

April 1835 I have been blocking out lasts. got 50 blocked out. Made one pair of fine calfskin shoes and three pair of over socks for the sisters. I covered a whip stalk for Jonathan Wood. sewed it after a different plan from common; took what is called the leather apron stick. It is the best way for puting on covers; it leaves it smoothe & even.

June 1835 Luther began to erect the frame on the great house to hang the bell on.

I fixed a loom. Put in 2 girts for the roller to run on front of the yarn beam. In the morning I began to fix the lathe so it will swing or beat up of its own heft. got out a piece to put on for the purpose.

Sept. 1835 Made a milking stool.

January 1836 I turned and finished off a cap paddle; also a bone-handle to put a needle in & a great board for cutting brims.

Feb. 1836 Made a taylors yard stick for (b.c.) and a couple of rules figured off.
I split out some basket stuff and set up a basket Indian fine

March 1836 I put a pair of rockers on a chair for Molly Bennett. I made a lathe to weave home brade with. I made a rolling machine to roll brade in. Made seven pencils of red chawk.

August 1836 I began to make myself a new desk for writing on:

> And so it is while time does last,
> I find enough to do;
> With busy hands can't work so fast,
> But what there's more to do.

December 1836. Made a pair of butternut serge shoes for Polly Reed

January 1837 I made a pair of cloth shoes, made two baches of wax.

February 1837 Commenced making a bonnet loom P.M. Have finished the frame to said loom & made the lathe today. Finished said loom and seat to set on. Reconing my time from the beginning I was just about a week amaking it. Today I took it over to the spinshop & set it a going. O. Gates weaves on it first.

April 1837 After two oclock I went up to the machine shop and made a beginning to match the boards for the sounding frame or leaf that is agoing to be swung overhead in the Meeting house to prevent the sound echoing.

May 1837 I turned 15 handles 12 which are for chisels, for Hiram & myself.

July 1837 I collected some stuff, or boards for a tool cupboard; and made a slant for Derobigne to write on; to fold up on his counter.

I made a cupboard to keep my tools in for joinery. I made a couple of peg drawers with its carcase to go on the head of my bench.

December 1837 After dinner I was called in the house to learn a new manner of dance that was given in vision at Watervliet by Mother Lucy.

May 1838 Set up a pleasant spinner for Eliza Sharp.

Dec. 1838 I worked up in the south garret making a vice-bench and fixed over a vice and put it up.

Sept. 1839 I made a moddle of the tapeloom box that shuttles run into to send to Groveland.

October 1839 I turned a set of awl hafts, knife handles & peging awl hafts. I finished off my awlhafts, put in the awls & fitted out two benches. I made a number of shoulders & heel kees to rubing up shoes. I made two new side pieces to the boxes on the springshuttle loom.

Feb. 1840 Derobigne & Elisha B. has been to work for the convenience of the herb business, having been to work about the business for 9 days past. Put up a number of shelves and made a counter 8 feet long with seven drawers in it & 2 cupboards; finished all but top board & doors.

March 1840 Finished blocking out lasts, 86 of them in all & all hard maple of the best quality.

July 1840 I finished making a counter for the Deaconeses with 12 drawers. took between 3 & 4 weeks work. At the close of this it was thought best for me to leave South garret and go down below in Levi's shop, and take the wheel business accordingly I did, and fix over Levi's old work bench and put some drawers under it.

August 1841 Isaac N. Youngs & I commenced making a turning lathe for the wheel business.

June 1845 I have made 12 spinning wheels and 3 patent heads.

Certain data have already been offered indicating that joiners, or mechanics capable of working in wood, were members of the society in its formative stage. This evidence is buttressed by the report of early travelers. Thus Thomas Brown, who first visited the Niskeyuna settlement in 1798, was impressed by their "skilled mechanics," venturing the information that many of the first Believers were "collected" because of their "mechanical ingenuity." When President Timothy Dwight of Yale sojourned at New Lebanon in 1799, the Shakers there had already achieved a local reputation for "manual skill." William Haskett, a bitter critic of the religion, admitted that "there has some men of genius appeared in the Society; some as literary, but the major part as mechanical geniuses." Scattered records also indicate that cabinetmaking was included among the earliest industries of such widely separated communities as Shirley, Massachusetts, and Union Village, Ohio.

Internal evidence of the early presence of a class of carpenter-joiners is afforded by the "bills" of tools which accompanied "discharges" of work-men from covenant membership. Seceders were granted clothing, a sum of money, and often personal property previously dedicated by them to the joint interest, in return for which they signed an agreement not to bring suit against the society for labor rendered. On the occasion of their discharges in 1796, tools were returned to two such craftsmen, Samuel Chapman (a wheelwright) and Benjamin Goodrich (a joiner), according to the following inventories:

SAMUEL CHAPMAN'S TOOLS

One Broad ax	£ 1	0	0		
1 Narrow Do	0	12	0		
1 Broad Hatchet	0	14	0		
1 Addi [adz?]	0	14	0		
6 Augers @ ¼ a quarter	1	8	8		
3 fraiming Chessels and guage	0	14	0		
3 pairing Chisels and guage	1	4	0		
one Pair Compasses [?]	0	6	0		
one squair	0	8	0		
3 turning Chisels and 3 guages	1	4	0		
2 Shaves	0	13	6		
1 pair Nippers	0	5	0		

Compas Saw 0 2 6
Bench Dog 0 1 0
Handsaw 0 16 1
Splitting gage, and Small Do 0 9 0
Jointer [joiners'?] Trying plain for plain smoothing 1 12 0
2 wooden Squairs & turning gages 0 4 0
3 mallets 0 4 0
one Spoke Sett 0 2 0
Chalk Roole [rule?] and Line 0 3 0
Glue pot 0 5 0
Board Rule 0 2 0
9 files 0 16 0
Gimblets and Brad Awls 0 2 0

2 formas [forms?] 2 Scribing Guages
one Duks bill [duck's bill] Chisel   0   6   8
Spoke knife   0   2   0
one nail punch   0   1   0
one nail hammer   0   9   0

3 guages and 8 files taken Back and the amount of them given in Breast wimble and Bits.

BENJAMIN GOODRICH'S TOOLS

3 Screw Augers 1½—1¼ & 1 inch in Size and 1 two inch do [ditto]

1 hand, one pannel, one fine and 2 Small fine Saws 5 in. ye Whole

1 pair framing Chizzels

one Shop Hatchet—1 Iron Squair

2 Jointers—1 fore plain—1 Smoothing plain—1 Cornish [cornice?]

1 Pannil plain [panel-plane]—1 Plow [?] with 3 Irons

3 Sash plains

1 pair Sash plains—1 Large and 1 Small Bead

2 Rabit plains—3 Quarter Rounds ½—⅜ & ¼ inch

1 more ¾ [Quarter Round]—1 halving plain

1 pair Inch hollows and Rounds—1 pair ¾ inch do.

1 pair ½ inch do—1 Small round—3 Gages—1 Bit stock.

1 Large and 1 Small Wooden Square—1 hand Hammer.

2 Duck bill Chizzels—1 Scribing Guage— 3 Bits & chocks

1 Trying plain.

One of the first converts to Shakerism in New Lebanon was Gideon Turner, who in 1788 consecrated to the use of the church "1 Set Carpenters tools & 1 Set Joiners Tools" valued at eight pounds. By 1789, the church was engaged in making "turning tools" of its own, and mechanical equipment was being manufactured or purchased to supply adequately the needs of every branch of industry. It was not from lack of means that the Shakers did not produce the most ornamental and intricate cabinetwork.

Data recorded elsewhere in this study confirm the fact that the Shakers made furniture before 1800. Chairs date back to 1789. Clocks and chests were produced in 1790. Trestle tables, weave-stands, benches and folding beds were almost certainly made immediately after the communities were organized. Of early origin were the tailoring counters, cobblers' benches, candlestands and tables with one-piece tops. Fine cabinetwork was likewise expended on the casings, doors, blinds and built-in drawers and cupboards of dwellings and meeting-houses erected during the last two decades of the eighteenth century. (See Plate 5.)

Specimens of this earliest cabinetwork may usually be recognized by their primitive design and the subtle proofs of antiquity. In the finishing of furniture, paint preceded the thin, red stains and later varnishes; wrought nails, screws and hinges indicate early workmanship; end cleats pegged or nailed into table tops were usually prior to the tongue-and-groove cleats; wide dovetailing was antecedent to the narrow, the lipped drawer to the flush, and so on. The age of chairs is roughly indicated by the type of seat, the shape and use of dowels, as well as by the general appearance. Certain types of furniture were introduced or improved at given periods in the history of the sect, while others became obsolete.

Such evidence, however, is usually an unreliable index of exact age. Ascription is always complicated by the tendency of all kinds of joinery to conform to persistent modes. "We find out by trial what is best," explained a novitiate elder at New Lebanon, "and when we have found a good thing . . . we stick to it." Furniture was also so well cared for that the lapse of decades was not accurately reflected in its outward aspect. Pieces were seldom inscribed, though the Millennial Laws allowed the use of "two figures for a date."

It is just as difficult to ascribe examples of furniture to given artisans. In the first place, the insistence on simplicity of form and conformity to convention limited the range of variation. Secondly, though in principle "individual taste" was left "rather free," in practice the artistic formulae of individual craftsmen were merged in the larger scheme of Shakerism itself. "I can see great importance in a principle," declared Elder Evans, "very little in an individual."* Socialization of interests involved humility and the submergence of self, in aspects of work as of life. In the Millennial Laws "Concerning the Marking of Clothes, Tools and Conveniences," the doctrine of self-abnegation is reflected and enforced in such rules as these:

THE initials of a person's name are sufficient mark to put upon garment, or tool, for the purpose of distinction.

It . . . is strictly forbidden unnecessarily to embellish any mark.

No one should write or print his name on any article of manufacture, that others may hereafter know the work of his hands.

It is not allowable for the brethren, to stamp, write, or mark, their own names, upon anything which they make for the sisters, nor for sisters to do in like manner upon articles made for the brethren.

Ye shall not mark work baskets, work boxes, spool stands, needle and other cushions, rulers, etc. Nor joiners and carpenters tools with the mark of individuals.

Doctrine and law could not completely alter the humanity of a Shaker "family," however, and traces are frequent of individual taste in workmanship as well as pride in possession. Though furniture could not be owned "as private property, or individual interest," pieces were sometimes made for a favorite brother's or sister's use and inscribed by the consignee, as a token of respect, with the date and maker's name or initials. The appended list of marked pieces, illustrative of this innocent aberration from the Shaker code, also lends documentary support to the contention that the first half of the nineteenth century was the productive period of "classic" Shaker furniture. Pieces dated after 1850 are rare.

1801. Armed four-slat rocking chair, New Lebanon. (Plate 16.) Old, apparently original label bearing the number (01) pasted on back of slat. The tops of the front posts of many early Hancock side chairs were impressed with arabic num-

*Evans, Frederic William. *Autobiography of a Shaker*, p. 9.

bers 13, 15, 16, 17, 19, etc., which evidently record the last two digits of a date. These figures are confined to the teens, disproving the theory that they were size or room numbers and indicating that a large proportion of Hancock chairs may have been produced during the second decade of the last century. The initials "F. W." enclosed in a scalloped border and impressed by a die on the front posts of other Hancock three-slats, refer, according to tradition, to the West family.

1806. Floor clock from Niskeyuna. The inscription, "Benjamin Youngs, Watervliet," is lettered on the dial. The date has been subsequently crayoned. Clockmakers seem to have been excepted from the rule which disapproved of labeling: both Benjamin and Isaac Youngs inscribed their full names and often the date on their timepieces.

1812. Cobbler's bench from South family, New Lebanon. Crayoned on the lower drawer bottom is the date, "January, 1812."

1813. Candlebox from Hancock. Date pricked on side.

1817. Pine case of drawers from the Second family, New Lebanon. Inscribed on the inside of a drawer is the record: "Made by A. B. 1817." Amos Bishop was a member of the family of John Bishop, who lived on the site of the South family at the time Mother Ann visited the town in 1783.

1817. Pine case of drawers with cupboard. Church family, New Lebanon. Inscribed on base of frame: "Aug. 29, 1817. J (?) B & G L." J. B may stand for John Bishop (d.1828) or Job Bishop. Among the Bishops were several cabinetmakers who probably produced many of the earliest pieces at New Lebanon. "Father" Job Bishop was sent from New Lebanon to organize the community at Canterbury, New Hampshire, where he continued to work at his trade of chair and cabinetmaking. The only "G. L." in the church's death-book up to 1849 was Garret Lawrence, a Shaker physician and botanist (d. 1837), who was instrumental in building up the medicinal herb industry at New Lebanon. This cupboard may possibly have been made for his shop use.

1817. Wall-clock made by Calvin Wells of Watervliet.

1826. Small pine cupboard, New Lebanon. The date and the name "William Trip" is written on the bottom of the drawer. Trip was born in 1809 and is listed as a member of the Second Order, Church family, in 1819. The date of death is not recorded, which probably means that he left the society.

1827. Earliest measuring-stick date. In 1825 the Shaker tailors began to work according to systematic principles, and in the next twenty to thirty years, fine pine and maple tailoring-sticks, often dated, were made in many patterns.

1830. Pine case of drawers with cupboard top. (See Plate 22.) New Lebanon church. Inscription on base of drawer: "Dec. 1830, made by Amos Stewart." Stained with a red wash or thin water paint.

Some of the finest cases of drawers and other pieces made at the parent society in the second quarter of the last century may safely be attributed to this elder. Amos was a brother of Philemon Stewart, author of that strange, professedly inspired work, "A Holy Sacred and Divine Roll and Book." Amos died March 7, 1884, at the age of 81.

1830. Small three-drawer counter. Pine, painted red. Inscribed on back: "A. W. 1830." Made for Anne Williams, an eldress at the South family, New Lebanon, where the case was found.

1833. Pine case of drawers with cupboard top, stained red. New Lebanon Church family. Inscription on bottom of small drawer just below cupboard: "March 27, 1833. Made by Orren H." (Orren Haskins.)

1837. One-drawer blanket-chest. Pine. (Plate 19.) An inscription burned into the back reads, "Made April, 1837. Canaan." Tradition ascribes the chest to Gilbert Avery, father of Elder Giles Avery. Gilbert was also a chair-maker. The two families at Canaan (New York) were branches of the North family at New Lebanon.

1838. Washstand from New Lebanon church, dated "Feb. 24, 1838."

1838. Writing-box or lap-desk from New Lebanon. Penciled on the drawer bottom is the record: "February 6th 1838 by Maker Orren N. Haskins. R. B." Probably a presentation piece to the owner (Rachel Bacon?) whose initials conclude the inscription.

1840. Wall-clocks made by Isaac N. Youngs. (Plates 16 and 42.) Each of the three recorded clocks by this maker is inscribed with the same date, even to the day of the month. Youngs made clocks as early as 1815.

1841. Writing-box from New Lebanon inscribed: "August 24, 1841. Elisha Blakeman." In a Civil War MS. Blakeman is listed as a mechanic. He was born in 1819.

1842. A late form of trestle table, with highly arched shoe, still in use at Canterbury. The year-date only is impressed on the longitudinal brace.

1843. Pine case of drawers with top cupboards. A varnished piece, but otherwise made in the same style as the 1830 example, probably by Amos Stewart.

1843. Tailoresses' counter, curly maple, from Hancock. The placard reads: "This table was moved into the Elder Sister's Room June 22, 1843." The piece is undoubtedly earlier.

1844. Pine chest of drawers from Shirley. Crayoned: "Built by Elder Joseph Myrick, 1844. Finished March 8. Shirley. Myra McLean."

1845. Pine chest of drawers from Harvard, similar to the Myrick piece. Inscribed with date only.

1849. Child's case of drawers, butternut. (Plate 20.) Marked: "Enfield, Conn. May 16, 1849. Abner Alley. A E. age 66."

A list of all the joiners and wood turners who made furniture in the eleven eastern societies between 1787 and the Civil War would include scores of obscure master joiners and their apprentices. Their personalities are lost in the depths of the cause they served, their occupations seldom recorded. Following are the names of the most important craftsmen at New Lebanon, and a very incomplete list for the other societies. To them all we may apply that eulogy, written at Canterbury after his death in 1899, to Elder Benjamin H. Smith, a craftsman of the later period: *Who so conscientious that all his handwork should keep close to the perfect pattern of the Master Workman,—who drew his affections in early days.**

Avery, Gilbert (1775–1853)
Avery, Giles (1815–1890)
Bennett, Henry (1779–1852)
Bishop, Amos (1780–1857)
Bishop, James (d. 1822)
Blakeman, Elisha (left society)
Calver, James (went to Florida)
Chapman, Samuel (no record)
Chase, Edward (left society)
DeWitt, Henry (1806–1855)
Ellis, Samuel (1760–1818)
Estes, Thomas (b. 1782)
Farnham, James (1784–1858†)
Gilman, Ransome (1813–1880)
Goodrich, Benjamin (left society)
Haskins, Orrin (Orren) (d. 1886)
Jewett, Amos (1753–1834)
Knight, Abel (d. 1842)

Lockwood, John (1791–1878)
Middleton, Clawson (Canaan)
Munson, Thomas (no record)
Osborne, Noah (1765–1813)
Shapley, John (d. 1812)
Slingerland, Joseph (died at South Union)
Stewart, Amos (1803–1884)
Talcott, Asa (d. 1822)
Thrasher, William (1796–1896)
Trip, William (no record)
Turner, Gideon, Sr. (d. 1815)
Turner, Gideon, Jr. (d. 1852)
Wagan, Robert (1833–1883)
Wickersham, George (1811–1891‡)
Wilson, James (went to Canaan)
Youngs, Isaac (1793–1865)

Cabinetmakers from other societies:

Allis (Ellis?), Abram (Watervliet)
Alley, Abner (Enfield, Conn.)
Battles, Albert (Tyringham)

Bishop, Job (Canterbury)
Blinn, Henry (Canterbury)
Brewster, Justus (Hancock)

*Wilson, Josephine E. *The Manifesto*, September, 1899, Vol. XXIX, No. 9, p. 134. "A Farewell to Elder Benjamin H. Smith."
†Another record gives 1857 as the date of death.
‡Also given as 1892.

Brooks, Lorenzo (Enfield, Conn.)
Chase, Nelson (Enfield, Conn.)
Coffin, John (Maine bishopric)
Corbett, Thomas (Canterbury)
Damon, Thomas (Hancock)
Fisher, Thomas (Enfield, Conn.)
Grover, Edward (Canterbury)
Hammond, Thomas (Harvard)
Johnson, Joseph (Canterbury)
Kidder, Eli (Canterbury)

Libbey, William (Canterbury)
Myrick, Joseph (Harvard)
Sawyer, Otis (Maine bishopric)
Smith, Benjamin (Canterbury)
Terry, David (Hancock)
Wells, Calvin (Watervliet)
Wilcox, George (Enfield, Conn.)
Woods, Joseph (Canterbury)
Wright, Grove (Hancock)
Youngs, Benjamin (Watervliet)

IV

SHAKER HOUSES AND SHOPS

Appreciation of Shaker craftsmanship involves more than the isolated examination of types or individual examples. More than ornate or sophisticated workmanship, the furniture of the Believers needs to be seen in its native setting, where one piece supplements another and the room itself completes the composition. Unconsciously, these people applied one of the cardinal principles of the modern American architect, Frank Lloyd Wright: "To incorporate as organic architecture—so far as possible—furnishings, making them all one with the building and designing them in simple terms. Again straight lines and rectilinear forms." Divorced from their natural background of white plastered walls, warm yellow floors and simply framed doors and windows, Shaker appointments lose some of the quiet elegance born of their religious use.

The details of architectural design, the organization of families in the community and the grouping of buildings within the family unit, lie outside the province of the present study. Sufficient to note that buildings were faithful expressions of the creed that form was dependent on function, that faith should be externalized in the work of the hands. The Holy Laws of Zion illuminate the ideal:

Do not be expensive and extravagant in your buildings; but modest and neat. For a lowly cottage, in order and cleanliness, is far more beautiful than a grand dwelling, made or inhabited by that which is unclean.

Was it not the pattern that was set by your first Parents . . . [who] laid the foundation for you to build upon, to be tidy and snug in temporal things? . . . and zealous to keep all things in order?

When there was a building to repair or be built, when the signal was given, all would lend a liberal hand, and feel an interested desire to see how quick it would be accomplished; loving to see all things in order, and knowing it would please their blessed parents; in so doing they obtained the blessing of God, and built up the Church in order and in beauty.

[Whatever is fashioned, let] it be plain and simple, and of the good and substantial quality which becomes your calling and profession, unembellished by any superfluities, which add nothing to its goodness or durability. Think not that ye can keep the laws of Zion while blending with the forms and fashions of the children of the unclean!

Labor until ye bring your spirits to feel satisfied, and thankful for that degree of modest plainness in all that you possess.

Like the furniture, Shaker dwellings evolved from the simple styles common in the New England countryside to a somewhat distinct structural type planned to meet the needs of community life. The typical house was large, severely plain but scrupulously neat. A belfry sometimes surmounted the hip roof, and separate doorways (often hooded) were provided for sisters and brethren. Double entrances also characterized the meeting-house, a building distinguished in the community by its gambrel roof and white paint. The dooryards, fences and roads were trim and orderly. "In architecture and neatness," wrote Robert Wickliffe, a Southern advocate, in 1831, "[the Shakers] are exceeded by no people upon the earth."*

It is with the interiors of such buildings, however, the style and appearance of the rooms, that we are more immediately concerned. In the first buildings erected, the rooms were not distinctive: the halls were narrow, the stairs steep and the rooms "very contracted." But with the growth of the institution, more commodious and systematic provision was made for the domestic life, the work and worship of the people. The size and arrangement of rooms; the provision for light and ventilation; the built-in drawers, cupboards, shelves, wood-boxes and side benches; the honest workmanship on casings, doors, banisters, floors and walls; the installation in rooms and halls, everywhere, of pegboards; the attention to restrained but useful detail—all expressed the conviction on the part of the builders that they "had a thousand years to live."

The disposition of rooms logically expressed the Believers' idea that the sexes should be equal but separate. The two entrances led into a dual

*The Shakers. Speech of Robert Wickliffe. In the Senate of Kentucky, January, 1831. Frankfort, Ky. 1832.

system of lower and upper halls, stairways and retiring-rooms.* The family meeting-room and dining hall were common gathering places, but in the former room two series of benches or chairs were placed opposite each other, and in the latter the sexes ate at separate tables. The basement floor was reserved for the kitchens, cellars and storerooms. The dining and meeting-halls were usually located on the first floor above, as were the rooms set apart for the family deacons and deaconesses, elders and eldresses. The top floor or loft was one large chamber, with cases of drawers built along the sides in long, neat rows. Small anterooms were sometimes partitioned off under the eaves. Deviation from this general pattern of arrangement was not uncommon, however, the same limited freedom being allowed in planning a building as in designing a table or chair.

The undated architect's plans for an early family dwelling at New Lebanon will illustrate one method of distributing rooms. In this manuscript,† the floors above the basement were divided by central halls seventy-two feet long and four feet, two inches wide. The basement hall separated two series of rooms: on one side the apple cellar, the deaconesses' cellar and the meat cellar; and on the other, the kitchen sisters' room, the pantry, the "little kitchen," a small dining room and the "milk and pie room." One end of this floor was completely occupied by the cook-room and the bake-room. Over these, on the first floor, was the main dining hall, measuring twenty-five by fifty feet. On one side of the passage in this "loft" were two "dormitories" for sisters, each room eighteen by twenty feet, and a sisters' gathering-room twenty by twenty-four feet. Corresponding accommodations for brethren occupied the other side. The family meeting-

---

*Sleeping rooms or dormitories were called "retiring-rooms" because it was to these chambers, on the ringing of a bell (at seven-thirty in the summer and eight in the winter) that the brethren and sisters retired a half-hour before evening worship. During this time the occupants of each room, usually numbering four to eight individuals, sat erect in their chairs, "in one or two ranks," laboring "for a true sense of their privilege in the Zion of God." If any one chanced to fall asleep during this period of meditation, "they may rise and bow four times, or gently shake, and then resume their seat." (Elkins, *op. cit.*, p. 25. See also: "Orders concerning the Spiritual Worship of God," "Attending to Meetings," etc., in the *Millennial Laws.*)

†MS. No. 500 in authors' library.

room, thirty by fifty feet, was on the second floor above the dining hall. The remainder of this floor and all of the third were occupied by sisters' and brethren's retiring-rooms, six on each floor. In another set of specifications,* the halls were nine feet wide, and special provision was made for the deacons and deaconesses on the first floor, and on the second for the family elders and eldresses. Some of the finest furniture, if such a distinction can be made, was reserved for the use of the "lead," especially the ministry, whose "dwelling place [was] in the meeting house, even the most holy sanctuary."

The principle of economy that governed the furnishing of these "churches, meeting-halls and retiring rooms" was thus defended by Elder Giles Avery: "If sacred places are abandoned to secular uses, cumbered with the truck of trade, papers, books, literature of a worldly character, or needless furniture inappropriate to a place of retirement and worship, there is unavoidably added much labor of obtaining, in those retreats, a heavenly, devotional, worshipful spirit; because of the sensitiveness of the human soul to surroundings."† In the great room of the meeting-houses, where the early Shakers danced and chanted and listened to the exhortations of their elders, the only furniture was the plain benches and stationary seats built in a single row along the wall, or in tiers on platforms at the side of the hall. Except for these rows of forms, it appeared like a large, empty hall, but clean and suffused with sanctity. For "everything that is attached either to the inside or the outside of such buildings and places [saith the Lord] should be perfect and plain, free from all unnecessary embellishments: for in this my last display of grace to man, I leave no room for halfway work, either in things inward or outward."‡ Before the advent of the organ, the meeting-room in the dwelling was no less simply furnished, though chairs or benches with backs had long supplanted the long backless forms.

Elder Giles's characterization of the retiring-room applied to the family dwelling as a whole. Through the day the house was vacated by all except

---

*MS. No. 501 in authors' library.

†Avery, G. B. "Sacred Places, Sacred Seasons." In *The Shaker Manifesto*, April, 1879, Vol. IX, No. 4, p. 74.

‡Stewart, Philemon. *A General Statement of the Holy Laws of Zion.*

those sisters appointed to kitchen duty, chamber work or housecleaning. An early writer records that

NONE shall go thither only for the purposes of eating, sleeping, retiring for evening worship, and spending the Sabbath, unless for short errands. . . . When brethren and sisters enter, they must uncover their heads and hang their hats and bonnets in the lower corridors, and walk softly and open and shut doors gently, and in the fear of God . . . In a word, the sanctuary, and the whole house, shall be kept sacred and holy unto the Lord; and all shall spend the time allotted for to be in the house, mostly in their own rooms.*

Though no contemporary record exists of the appearance of a furnished retiring-room during the first half-century of Shaker history, imaginative reconstruction is possible on the basis of architectural background, the character of the furniture itself, the regulations on furniture drawn up in the 1840's, and finally, the observations by travelers of interiors which had remained virtually unaltered for decades. The same qualities which mark the furniture of the Believers are immediately suggested by the physical aspect and atmosphere of a spacious though empty present-day room. The white ceiling and walls, whose polished surface is broken only by the lines of pegs or an occasional row of built-in drawers, reflect and augment the light from large, spotlessly clean windows. In the shops it was customary to use white shades, which were attached to rollers inserted in small, elongated pegs set into the hard plaster and provided at one end with a large, grooved wheel around which passed a regulatory cord fastened to a fixture below. Paneled blinds, or blinds with shutters set at a fixed angle, were often used on dwelling houses and churches, rendering shades unnecessary; though sometimes half-curtains were used, blue or green or white. The doors and casings, of yellow pine, were oiled to a soft yellow-brown, and the floors stained a harmonizing "reddish-yellow." The window sashes could be easily lowered or raised, and were so designed that by removing a side-strip fastened by wooden screws, the sashes could be removed and conveniently cleaned. Ventilation was further insured by small holes along the baseboards of the halls, or by perforated panels set into the baseboards or doors.

The earliest attempt to regulate the furnishing of retiring-rooms is

*Elkins, *op. cit.*, p. 26.

found in an inspirational message received by the instrument, Anna Dodgson of New Lebanon, from the Holy Angel of the Lord, through Father Joseph Meacham. Recorded August 12, 1841, the following references to "suitable furniture for dwelling rooms" suggest what such chambers may have contained for a long period previous to this date:

GREEN painted bed steads; plain chairs, with splint bottoms are preferable to any other kind, because they can be mended when they break. One rocking Chair, in a room, except where the aged reside. One table, or more, if necessary, according to the number of inmates and size of the room. One stand.

One good looking glass, which ought not to exceed eighteen inches in length, and twelve or fourteen in width, with a frame one inch and a half wide. . . . If another glass is really necessary, have a smaller one, and hang it in the closet. A little glass, perhaps eight or ten inches square, may be placed in every room, but no particular one ought to own a looking glass of any size whatever.

Carpets are admissable but they ought to be used with discretion, and made plain. Mother Lucy says two colours are sufficient for one Carpet. Make one stripe of red and green, another of drab and grey, another of butternut and grey. The binding yarn may also be of two colours, and also the binding if necessary.

One good glass Lamp to be provided for every room, if more are needful, as often is the case, let them be provided in order for the room. But I hope I shall never hereafter see any of my brethren or Sisters carrying a lamp, from room to room, or hear the word spoken, "My glass Lamp."!

Three good clothes brushes, I think are sufficient, for any room, and if there are any held in possession by individuals, they ought to be given up to supply places where more are needed.

No drawers, chests, nor cupboards, ought to be put in the lower halls of the dwelling house. But they may be placed in the other halls if necessary.*

The Millennial Laws of 1845 give the following Orders Concerning Furniture in Retiring Rooms:

THE following is the order in which retiring rooms should be furnished: the number of articles may be more, or less, according to the size of the room and the number of inmates therein.

Bedsteads should be painted green—Comfortables should be of a modest color. Blankets for outside spreads should be blue and white, but not checked or striped; other kinds now in use may be worn out.

*"The Word of the Holy Angel of the Lord, to Father Joseph. Father's Word." February 14, 1841. Inst. Anna Dodgson. Recorded August 12, 1841.

One *rocking chair* in a room is sufficient, except where the aged reside. One table, one or two stands, a lamp stand may be attached to the wood work if desired. One good looking glass, which ought not to exceed eighteen inches in length, and twelve in width, with a plain frame. A looking glass larger than this, ought never to be purchased by Believers. If necessary a small glass may hang in the closet, and a very small one may be kept in the public cupboard of the room.

Window curtains should be white, or of a blue or green shade, or some very modest color, and not red, checked, striped or flowered.

The carpets in one room should be as near alike as can consistently be provided, and these the Deaconesses should provide.

No maps, Charts, and no pictures or paintings, shall ever be hung up in your dwelling rooms, shops, or Office. And no pictures or painting set in frames, with glass before them, shall ever be among you. But modest advertisements may be put up in the Trustees Office when necessary.

If any person or persons, mar, break, or destroy, any article or articles of furniture in the retiring rooms, it is such an one's duty to acknowledge the same to the Deacons or Deaconesses, as the case may be, and if possible to repair the injury.

No allusion is made in the above statutes to side chairs, desks, clocks, stoves or washstands, all of which are mentioned by Elkins or other writers. No ruling could be made on chairs, as the number depended on how many sisters or brethren were assigned to a given room. A drop-leaf table, or table with one-piece top, was used for writing as well as for holding books and the lamp, all but lap-desks being reserved for the family "leads." Clocks were also prohibited in common members' rooms. Each chamber had its own little stove, of quaint Shaker manufacture, the narrow, elbowed pipe leading into a central flue. A long tin "smoker" or "lily," shaped at one end like a funnel, carried the smoke or gas from the candles and lamps into a single flue. Adjoining the chamber was often an anteroom furnished with a washstand, towel rack and cot. (See Plate 40.) This extra room sometimes took the form of a clothespress provided with a complete housekeeping equipment.

Everywhere was evidence that Mother Ann's admonition against "costly and extravagant furniture" was religiously obeyed. Since "all unnecessary and superfluous articles of furniture were avoided," the New Lebanon trustees reported, in 1850, that "the actual cost of furnishing one of our dwellings for the comfortable accomodation of 60 or 70 inmates would fall far short of the sum often expended in furnishing some single parlors in the cities of New-York and Albany."* In the long halls, the passages and stairways, the attic lofts and basements, the meeting- and dining halls, no dispensable object or discordant note broke the primitive rhythm of line and mass and soft colors. Such was the reverence of the Shakers for useful hand labor that occupational scenes, too—the nurse-shop, the weave-shop, the schoolroom, the office—had the same air of ordered frugality, with no concession to inconvenience or unloveliness, which prevailed in the communal dwelling or meeting-house. The aspect was one of "perennial nobleness, and even sacredness," into which blended the unhurried movement of the people, the silence at meals, the meditation and hush of a perpetual Sabbath.

From a number of accounts of Shaker scenes, made during the last century, a few have here been selected as a possible aid to visualizing the old interiors, though most such observations, we must remember, came after the Civil War, when the retiring-rooms in particular had begun to lose a little of their extreme plainness. As early as 1839, however, Harriet Martineau wrote that the Believers had the "best" furniture, as well as the best crops, medicines, house-linen, roads, fences and habitations in the country. . . . "The frame-dwellings, painted straw-colour, and roofed with deep-red shingles, were finished with the last degree of nicety, even to the springs of the windows and the hinges of the doors. The floors were as even and almost as white as marble."†

In 1844, another traveler, John Finch, observed that

EACH of these communities is a well-built, handsome village, with wide streets laid out regularly at right angles; the houses, factories, workshops, agricultural buildings, and public halls, are all large and well built; these are surrounded with beautiful and well cultivated kitchen and flower gardens, vineyards, orchards, and farms, the very best that are to be seen in the United States; their horses, their cows and their sheep, are some of the best bred and best fed that I ever saw; their long ranges of stacks of grain, well filled barns, and well filled stores, prove that they have neither want nor the fear of it. The neatness, cleanliness and order which you everywhere observe in their persons and their premises, and the cheerfulness and contented looks of the people, afford the reflective mind continual

---

*State of New York. (Document) No. 89. In Senate, March 19, 1850, pp. 6–7. (Report of the Shaker trustees at New Lebanon.)

†Baker, Arthur. *Shakers and Shakerism.* "New Moral World" Series, pp. 18–19.

pleasure; here none are overworked, and none ever want a day's labour; none live in luxury, and no man, or woman, or child, lacks anything.*

In *Fifteen Years in the Senior Order of Shakers*, Hervey Elkins gave an intimate picture and interpretation of Shaker life. According to this account, the retiring-rooms (at Enfield, New Hampshire) were "all exactly twenty feet square, nine feet high, and of identical furniture and finish, rendering it difficult to determine, but by the number, one room from another." The furniture was also uniform:

THE dwelling rooms are strictly furnished according to the following rules: plain chairs, bottomed with rattan or rush, and light so as to be easily portable; one rocking chair is admissible in each room, but such a luxury is unencouraged; one or two writing tables or desks; one looking glass, not exceeding eighteen inches in length, set in a plain mahogany frame; an elegant but plain stove; two lamps; one candle-stick, and a smoker or tin funnel to convey to the chimney the smoke and gas evolved from the lights; bedsteads painted green; coverlets of a mixed color, blue and white; carpets manufactured by themselves, and each containing but three colors; two or three bibles and all the religious works edited by the Society, a concordance, grammar, dictionary, etc. These are all the books they tolerate in the mansion where they retire from labor and worldly pursuits. No image or portrait of anything upon the earth . . . is suffered in this holy place.†

Charles Nordhoff, in his survey of American communities in the early 1870's, was one of many to appreciate the cleanliness and order of Shaker domestic economy:

IF you are permitted to examine these shops and the dwelling of the family [he wrote], you will notice that the most scrupulous cleanliness is every where practiced; if there is a stove in the room, a small broom and dust-pan hang near it, and a wood-box stands by it; scrapers and mats at the door invite you to make clean your shoes; and if the roads are muddy or snowy, a broom hung up outside the outer door mutely requests you to brush off all the mud or snow. The strips of carpet are easily lifted, and the floor beneath is as clean as though it were a table to be eaten from. The walls are bare of pictures; not only because all ornament is wrong, but because frames are places where dust will lodge. The bedstead is a cot, covered with the bedclothing, and easily moved away to allow of dusting and sweeping. Mats meet you at the outer door and at every inner door. The floors of the halls and dining-room are polished until they shine.

Ibid., p. 22.
†Elkins, *op. cit.*, pp. 25–26, 39–40.

Moreover all the walls, in hall and rooms, are lined with rows of wooden pegs, on which spare chairs, hats, cloaks, bonnets, and shawls are hung; and you presently perceive that neatness, order, and absolute cleanliness rule every where.*

William Hepworth Dixon, editor of the *Athenæum* and author of *New America*, thus described the room assigned to him at the North family at New Lebanon:

My room is painfully bright and clean. No Haarlem vrouw ever scraped her floor into such perfect neatness as my floor; nor could the wood, of which it is made, be matched in purity except in the heart of an uncut forest pine. A bed stands in the corner, with sheets and pillows of spotless white. A table on which lie an English Bible, some few Shaker tracts, an inkstand, a paper-knife; four cane chairs, arranged in angles; a piece of carpet by the bedside; a spittoon in one corner, complete the furniture. A closet on one side of the room contains a second bed, a washstand, a jug of water, towels; and the whole apartment is light and airy, even for a frame house. . . . Stoves of a special pattern warm the rooms in winter, with an adjustment delicate enough to keep the temperature for weeks within one degree of warmth. Fresh air is the Shaker medicine.†

An interested visitor at the Shirley community was William Dean Howells, who based his *The Undiscovered Country* on the inspirational phenomena of the Shaker religion. In an article contributed to the *Atlantic Monthly* in 1876, he wrote as follows:

In each village is an edifice known as the Dwelling-House, which is separate from the office and the other buildings. In this are the rooms of the brothers and sisters, the kitchen and dining-room, and a large room for family meetings. The first impression of all is cleanliness, with a suggestion of bareness which is not inconsistent, however, with comfort, and which comes chiefly from the aspect of the unpapered walls, the scrubbed floors hidden only by rugs and strips of carpeting, and the plain, flat finish of the wood-work. Each chamber accommodates two brothers or two sisters, and is appointed with two beds, two rocking-chairs, two wash-stands, and a wood-stove, with abundance of rugs. . . . In the kitchen was an immense cook-stove, with every housekeeping convenience; and everywhere opened pantry and store-room doors, with capacious cellars underneath—all scoured and scrubbed to the last degree of neatness.‡

---

*Nordhoff, Charles. *The Communistic Societies of the United States*, pp. 136–137.

†Dixon, William Hepworth. *New America*, pp. 308–309.

‡Howells, William Dean. In the *Atlantic Monthly*, June, 1876, p. 709.

The unitary homes at Canterbury attracted the attention of a writer in the *Granite Monthly*, A. B. Harris, from whose article, written in 1877, the following excerpts are taken:

THEY [the Shakers] are there to stay. And that fact accounts for a great deal. It is partial explanation of the contentment on the faces of the Shaker sisters. It is a reason for the repose and settledness which pervade a Shaker village—that indefinable something, so altogether unlike the life of ordinary villages, and which you feel in the air, and are conscious of by some instinct, as men claim to be aware of the presence of spirits. Whether you pass along the streets, or enter the houses, or wherever you go, you feel that you are beyond the realm of hurry; there is no restlessness, or fret of business, or anxiety about anything; it is as if the work was done, and it was one eternal afternoon. Nor does anything dispel this feeling, even when you are in the midst of their industries, and the making of cheese, the milking of cows, the washing and ironing, and baking, and harvesting are going on around you. They do it all so leisurely, so quietly, that you feel something as he did who saw men "as trees walking" . . .

If one's preconceived idea about the rooms is that they are unattractive, by reason of the austerity in furnishing, and the general primness—that is altogether a mistake. There is an esthetic, as well as a very practical side. But it is by no means certain that it is not the latter which most readily takes the eye of the visitor who has ever had a house of her own. To such, there is refreshment in the absolute cleanliness and tidiness, and order. It is the one kind of household life where the rule of having "a place for everything, and everything in its place," is always carried out. The consummate result has there been reached. Everything runs smoothly. Evidently those who planned the domestic arrangements, while they had in view handiness and compactness, did not overlook the fact that there might be a great saving of noise and labor in the construction of furniture; and so, as far as practicable, they had presses and heavy benches built into the wall, instead of movable fixtures.*

And in our own day, of a room retaining its original character and furnished typically, a visitor thus records his impression:

HERE [at the Shaker settlement of Hancock near Pittsfield] I was permitted to view one of the least ostentatious but yet most singularly appealing rooms that I have ever entered. White as moonlight I remember its walls, white the plain linen curtains at the window, and against this pure background a few pieces of warm-toned nutwood furniture, soberly demure, yet without a hint of severity.

*Harris, A. B. *Among the Shakers*, pp. 21–22.

On a bed in the corner a blue homespun coverlet of wool was neatly spread; braided rugs patterned the floor with ovals of soft color. Near the centre of the room a chair stood beside a small round table, on which a single candle shone like the eye of innocence. An inexpressible atmosphere of quietude and peace pervaded the place, relaxing taut nerves like some beneficent opiate, and for the moment obscuring all realization of the tumultuous world outside. Spirits of just men made perfect—perhaps they were still abiding there in the calm silence. To me, at least, they seemed to surround like tangible presences.*

Emanating from a Shaker room of the older time is an air of serenity, humility and holiness—qualities medieval yet bright and in a sense modern; otherworldly, yet firmly fixed in a temporal plan. The sense is nevertheless strong of being above or beyond the familiar, the world as we know it, in an atmosphere purified, as it were, from the nonessentials of living—an intangible feeling difficult to describe. In a house that stands for the purest Shaker ideas on architecture, craftsmanship and domestic economy, we can be certain only that this is all part of a people's spiritual experience, and that the work of the hand exemplifies the beauty of labor dedicated to a church of Christ. It is a form of monasticism transferred to the New England scene.

*Keyes, Homer Eaton. In the magazine *Antiques*, October, 1934, pp. 146, 148.

V
CONCLUSION

THE strength and purity of the Shaker spirit, as expressed in its literature and ritual and work, were constantly in conflict with the forces of worldliness. For nearly a century this struggle was successfully waged. Separation of the sexes, separation from the world and separation from sin were maintained by the afflatus attendant on religious conviction, by the strength of tradition, by the efficient operation of the Millennial Laws. It was a century of medieval consecration, of mysticism, of the dominance of the spiritual over the material. Yet Shakerism was after all an isolated human institution, one of a multitude of sects, and not a branch, like the monasteries, of a strong ecclesiastical system. About the time of the Civil War, signs were evident of a gradual disintegration of the early unspoiled culture. The temper of the age was changing; conversions diminished; opportunity lured many away; and worldly industry, aided by the machine, overwhelmed the Shaker economy. It was necessary to hire more and more of the world's people to carry on the farm and shop operations initiated when handwork had a chance to compete in the market. As the "world" thus disturbed the Shaker order, it was increasingly difficult to maintain the tenets of the faith.

Leaders in the society foresaw and warned against this catastrophe. *The Manifesto*, the official organ of Shaker thought, pointed out that "when the Quakers so far forgot their union that they wrangled about doctrine, they sank into worldings"; and when the Methodists, "tired of their plainness ran after the fashions of the world, they no longer had spiritual gifts, nor came under the influence of the power of God." The Lord's witnesses, wrote another contributor (Elder John Vance), have been the "ascetics," traveling "the path of self-denial . . . while the falling away from every spiritual epoch has been marked by the ascendency of the asthetics [sic]." The forces of deception are all around:

> "Your house is too plain," said the proud old world,
>   "I'll build you one like mine;
> Carpets from Brussells and curtains of lace,
>   And furniture ever so fine."

The Shakers should "best love the beauty that is adapted to (their) condition," this elder concludes: that beauty which is "peculiar to the flower, or generative period," and not that "which belongs to the ripened fruit and grain."

Though the particular way of life adopted by the first Believers has never wholly broken down, though certain traditions have been tenaciously followed, and though many individuals (notably the aged) represent, even today, the spirit of the early sect, it is abundantly evident that secularism has changed the old order. Of particular interest is the effect of this change on craftsmanship. Little furniture (except chairs) was produced after the Civil War, and what was made often exhibited a marked reaction against that "plainness" with which the members of the society were once so satisfied. A case in point is the work of Thomas Fisher, a Scotch convert at Enfield, Connecticut, whose prolific output is marked by the decadent designs of Victorianism: designs which, sadly enough, were often preferred by latter-day Shakers to the fine simplicity of the traditional forms. As noted in the preface to this study, a distinct tendency existed toward compensation, and members were allowed to express their taste, naturally uncultivated and still restricted, for ornament and display in various forms. But as compromises were made with principle, the crafts inevitably deteriorated. The spiritual energy which went into the creative work of the early order was becoming constantly devitalized, and soon the point was reached where there could be no returning to the significant workmanship of the past.*

The furniture made by the Believers has more than a historic or anti-

---

*The cumulative effect of the early industriousness in the crafts was such that furniture making did not cease immediately after the society had reached its zenith of prosperity and started its slow numerical decline. Joiners like Amos Stewart of New Lebanon continued to make occasional pieces according to the strict conventions of the past. Many of the rocking chairs made by Robert Wagan found their way into Shaker homes, where they supplemented the relatively few old-type rockers—a concession to ease and comfort which in itself was significant. It soon became apparent, however, that the supply of furniture was more than adequate. Shops were closed, or used only for intermittent repairing or the production of accessories, and energies were almost wholly diverted to agriculture or horticulture. The Shaker school of craftsmanship was virtually extinct a half-century or more ago.

quarian value. It can be produced again, never as the inevitable expression of time and circumstance, yet still as something to satisfy the mind which is surfeited with over-ornamentation and mere display. More and more, in America, will there be people with limited means but educated taste, who will want their homes free from the complexity of useless embellishment, who will seek a union of practical convenience and quiet charm. Simple essential needs, not the whims of commercial manufacturers or the economy of overproduction, will increasingly dictate the kind and quantity of furniture to be used. Such furniture, like that made in the early Shaker settlements, will be flawless but inexpensive. It will satisfy all requirements, as it did among the Believers, whose communal homes demanded a diversity of appointments. Undue surface decoration or plastic embellishment, householders will find, not only adds to the cost, but conceals or distracts attention from the essential dignity of purely expressed forms. The dawning recognition of the possibilities of simplified workmanship and architectural setting lends hope that the cult will be more widely adopted, not as a gesture of exclusiveness or smartness, but as one of the best possible means of creating a serenely beautiful domestic environment.

Of great potential value, too, is the Shaker example of self-sufficiency and the full utilization of resources. They were, above all, workers in wood. That they loved this native material and took great pride in fashioning it to countless ends, is evidenced not only by the excellence of their craftsmanship and the variety of their achievement, but by the fact that long after prosperity came as the inevitable result of honest industry, they persisted in producing by hand labor an endless number of things which could more easily have been purchased in the markets of the world. The exaltation of handwork, aided but never usurped by the machines, was the Shaker ideal to which William Morris, and in this day, many another would return. And with it, conscience: not necessarily the particular conscience that Mother Ann exhorted her followers to foster in their souls, but a kindred sense of obligation, an awareness of standards, a desire to achieve perfection, a feeling for fitness and for form.

In the foreword to the first covenant adopted by the Second family at New Lebanon, it was written that

WHEN man by transgression lost his primitive rectitude, he then lost the unity of his true interest, both to God and his fellow creatures. Hence he became selfish and partial in all his views and pursuits. Instead of feeling it his interest and happiness to honor and build up the cause of God, and benefit his fellow creatures, his feelings were turned to exalt and build up himself at the expense of the peace and happiness of his own species, and the loss of his union to his Creator.

It is the sense of elemental rectitude, regained and transmitted to the things wrought by the hand, that the Shakers leave as no small part of their legacy.

THE PLATES

THE Shaker rooms in which the following photographs were prepared* belong to a period when furniture was none too common. Forced economy often predominated over convenience. Historic incorrectness, therefore, was not involved in eliminating from each composition extraneous material; nor do the formalities of arrangement conflict with the somewhat stark, austere effect which the early interiors must have presented. The selection of certain pieces for certain studies was indeed sometimes arbitrary. And though the placement of objects followed the ordinary rules of pictorial technique, every effort was made to evoke the spirit of the original scene, as we imagined it must be; to suggest in particular the historic order, cleanliness and spaciousness of the domestic scheme; to give a panorama of essential design, with a minimum of accessories; and in general to indicate both the atmosphere and practical economy of the Shaker home.

About half of the illustrations were taken in the sisters' shop or washhouse at the Church family, New Lebanon, two rooms on the third loft of which were cleared and restored to their original appearance. The large, well-lighted rooms of this building, which was raised on May 22, 1806, offered a faithful background for the portrayal of the authors' collection. The walls were rewhitened and the floors repainted. The pegboards and door and window casings were in good condition. Available also were the original window shades and rollers, with their ingenious fixtures. Under the sills were strips of tiny pegs on which tools, brushes or other objects were once hung. One of the rooms had a spacious anteroom or washroom, large enough to hold an extra cot and washstand. Various locations in the meeting-house at Hancock, and in the shops and dwellings at Hancock and New Lebanon, were utilized for the rest of the pictures, and are noted in the description of the Plates, pages 67 to 101.

*The authors wish to acknowledge their indebtedness to Mr. William F. Winter, of Schenectady, New York, whose skill as a photographer, high artistic standards and understanding of the Shaker theme itself were invaluable aids to truthful interpretation.

2

3

4

5

6

7

8

9

10

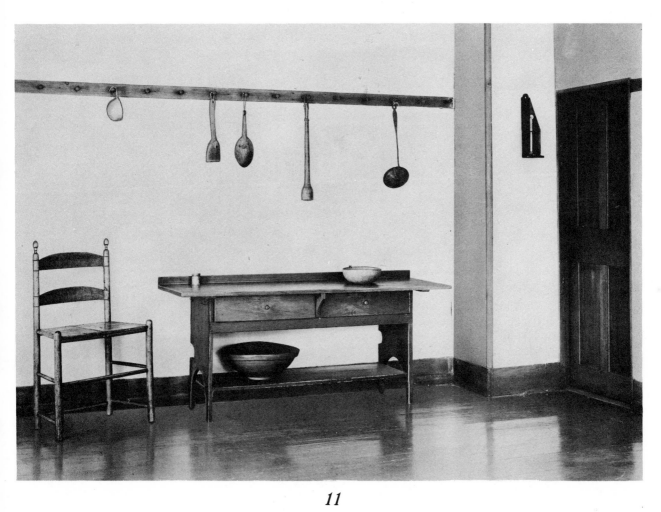

11

12

13

14

15

16

17

18

19

20

21

22

23

24

25

26

27

28

29

30

31

32

33

34

35

36

37

38

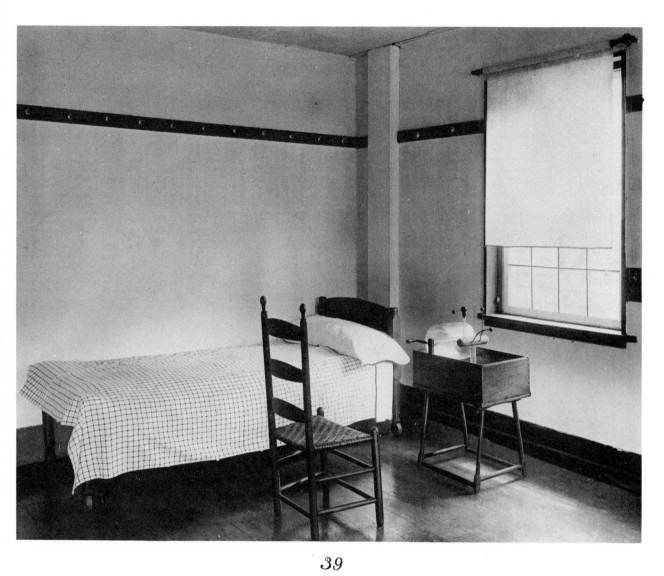

39

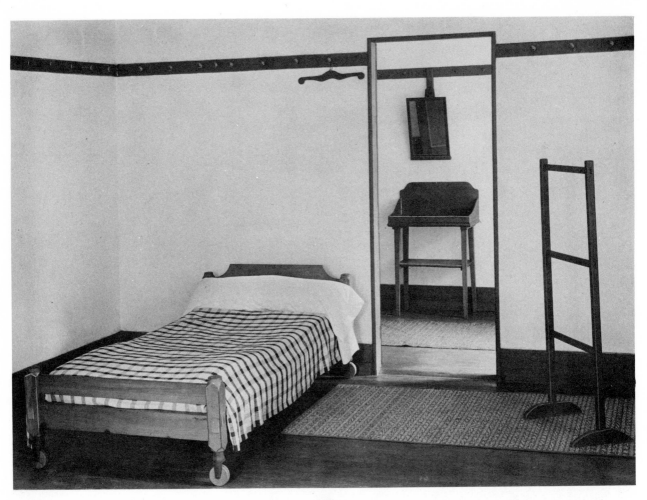

40

41

42

43

44

45

46

47

48

DESCRIPTIONS
TABLES, CHAIRS AND BENCHES*
PLATES 1–11

WHEN Ann Lee visited various towns in Massachusetts and Connecticut in 1783, she must have entered many homes reflecting in their furniture and decoration the feeling of self-importance which marked the development of middle-class consciousness during the eighteenth century. In such houses were frequent evidences of imported English and Continental taste: carved, inlaid, veneered, lacquered and painted furniture; special-service pieces like tea, card or dressing tables, symbolical of social pleasures; fine appointments such as high-boys, lowboys and chests-on-chests, desks and secretaries, settees or chaise longues, high-post beds, gilt mirrors and pier tables; chairs upholstered in velvets, damasks, satins and plushes; pretentious carpets, tapestries, wallpapers, table linens and silver. Ornament in many forms accompanied prosperity into the better New England homes, furnishing ready occasion for testimonials against the "worldly" temper of the age. At Petersham, in Massachusetts, Ann's dissenting spirit seized upon the subject of such "costly and extravagant furniture," the possession of which she utterly condemned as sinful indulgence. "Never put on silver spoons for me nor tablecloths," she directed in one of the homes of this town; "but let your tables be clean enough to eat on without cloths; and if you do not know what to do with them, give them to the poor."†

PLATE 1 (*Frontispiece*)
Ministry's dining room, with early trestle table and benches

SMALL trestle table from Enfield, Connecticut. The two-board top, of close-grained maple, measures 50 inches by 27 inches. Legs also of hard maple. Height: 24¾ inches.

The pine benches represent common types at New Lebanon. The one near the table measures 48 inches by 9¾ inches by 15¾ inches; the other: 40 inches by 9½ inches by 18½ inches. All boards are ⅞ inch thick, except those used for the top and braces of the lower bench, which are of ¾-inch stock. The tin candle sconce (from Hancock) is provided with a rack for matches or matchbox.

---

*Since seats of all kinds (chairs, benches, high stools, etc.) have a functional relationship with tables and are organic parts of most of the illustrations of table types, these various classes of furniture are described together as they appear in successive pictures. (See index for references.)

Tables, stands, case-furniture, etc. are measured below in the sequence: length by width by height.

† *Testimonies of the life, character, revelations and doctrines of our ever blessed mother Ann Lee*, pp. 267–268. Even today Shakers seldom use tablecloths. The tables at Enfield, N.H., in the middle of the last century were typical pieces: "long, three feet in width, polished high, without cloth." (*Fifteen Years in the Senior Order of Shakers*, pp. 24–25.)

The Shaker search for purity of form is well exemplified in the trestle dining-room tables made at an early date in the history of the order. Well adapted to communal use, such pieces possess an elemental character of dignity and frankness enhanced by flawless construction. In contrast with their colonial analogues, which the Shakers probably never saw, the longitudinal underbraces of these tables usually run directly beneath the top, leaving an unobstructed space for legs and knees. The top is pinned or nailed to this piece as well as to the cross-strips, and the underbrace is tenoned through the top of the leg-posts and wedged for tightness. On the earliest tables, the uprights of the trestles are urn-shaped (as in Plate 1), square or rectangular posts (generally maple), while the foundation shoes (maple, oak or ash) rest flush with the floor or are slightly arched in a long, bow-shaped curve. Later types are usually distinguishable by turned leg-posts and narrower feet or shoes. Cherry took the place of maple and pine; the length became standardized at ten feet and the width at three; and the shoes were raised to a higher arch.

The short trestle tables were made for the two elders and two eldresses composing the ministry, who ate apart from the rest of the society. Special care was often taken in making furniture consigned to this highest order of Shakerdom.

PLATE 2
Long communal dining table with benches

DIMENSIONS of table: 20 feet by 34 inches by 27⅛ inches. The four-board top is pine; the trestles, birch. The ten-foot benches in the picture were more often used in the meeting-house than in the dining hall, where shorter benches were more convenient to move. (See Plate 1.) All pieces from New Lebanon.

To facilitate passing of dishes, Shaker dining tables were set to accommodate one or more "squares" of four persons each. Ten-foot tables usually served three squares. The twenty-foot trestle table in Plate 2, made at New Lebanon, could accommodate twenty persons. The Believers ate their meals in monastic silence, the brethren and sisters at separate tables. Woodenware and pewter were used until the end of the first quarter of the last century, when they were succeeded by earthen and "white ware." The colloquialism, "Shaker your plate," dates from an early monition on table economy derived from Christ's injunction: "Gather up the fragments that remain, that nothing be lost."

PLATE 3
Community dining table and early dining chairs

THE trestle table has a pine, four-board top and maple uprights and shoes. Edges of the posts chamfered. Originally the top had no end cleats. Dimensions: 96 inches by 28¼ inches. All pieces from Hancock.

The chairs are maple throughout. In the one-slat type, the average distance from the top of the slat to the floor is 25 inches, and from the seat to the floor, 15¾ inches. The width at the front of the seat (measuring to the outside of the posts) is 17¼ inches, and at the back of the seat, 13 inches. In the two-slat type, the average distance from the top of the upper slat to the floor is 26 inches. The seats tend to slope slightly, averaging 16¼ inches from the floor in front and 15¾ inches in back. These chairs are also a little broader than the one-slats, the average width being 18½ inches in front and 14¼ inches at the back of the seat. After meals, or when the floor was being cleaned, the chairs were pushed under the table or hung on the pegboard.

Most of these low dining chairs were made at the Hancock or West Pittsfield community, though later types, with somewhat higher seats and of different woods, have been discovered at New Lebanon, Watervliet, Canterbury and Groveland; and a few common side chairs with two widely separated slats were produced at Harvard. The Hancock chairs were first used after the pine forms were discarded, the double-slat replacing the one-slat type, which provided insufficient support for the back. The two-slat chairs are equipped with wooden balls inserted in sockets at the bottoms of the back posts. (See Plate 45.)

PLATE 4

Side chairs arranged for a "union meeting"
THE chairs in Plate 4 are "tilting-chairs" made at Hancock. The rug was woven at New Lebanon. The clock is apparently a product of Isaac Youngs's early years at the latter colony. (See Appendix.)

First inaugurated in 1793, union meetings were features of Shaker domestic life for a century. On the three evenings of the week not devoted to religious meetings, a number of brethren would gather in a brethren's retiring-room, where they were joined by the same number of sisters. After placing themselves in rows "distant a few feet" from each other, the two sexes conversed "simply . . . on any subject connected with their home and religious life."

The apartness of the brethren's chairs (at left of picture) from the slightly lower ones occupied by the sisters is symbolical of the separateness of the sexes in Shaker

life. Many "separation acts" among the early, unprinted laws of the sect were the logical result of the belief in celibacy, in the principle that sex was sin. It was "contrary to order," for instance, for "a brother to pass a sister on the stairs" or for "a sister to go to the brother's shop, alone." Brethren and sisters could not "go into each other's rooms after evening meetings" or "talk together in the halls." Brethren could not "shake hands or touch the sisters . . . make any presents to the sisters . . . [or] go into the room when the sisters are making the beds." A brother and sister could not "eat at one table, unless there is company . . . ride together in a wagon without company," carry on any occupation, such as milking, together, or "be in a room together without company."

PLATE 5

Long meeting-house benches
TYPICAL meeting-house benches are 10 feet long, 11 inches wide and 16 inches high. Top planks are 1⅜ inches thick; leg-boards, 1¼ inches. Note the paneling of the window casings and the wall and window moldings. The extra lines of pegs were for the convenience of visitors.

Benches or forms of pine preceded chairs in the early Shaker dining halls, and persisted in the meeting-houses until late in the last century. The oldest ones date back to the first years of communal organization, when chairs were too uncommon to accommodate the large numbers assembling for meals or Sabbath worship. Most of the long eight- or ten-foot benches were used in meeting-rooms and churches. On them the Believers rested from the excitement of their rituals, or sat to listen to the harangues of the elders. They also accommodated the "world's people" who came to witness the singular mode of worship practised by the Shakers.

The common New Lebanon bench had a heavy plank top and two or three legs cut at the base in a round or Gothic arch and securely braced with strips half-dovetailed into the edge of the top board. Pieces with lighter tops, sometimes molded along the rim, were also common. In a Watervliet type, also seen in other communities, the legs were braced by double-ogee or butter-fly-wing supports, and occasionally by two neatly turned, parallel stretchers penetrating the leg-boards and secured on the outside by small pins. In many long benches, and often in the shorter ones, the leg-boards were mortised and wedged into the top, Windsor-fashion, and the medial-brace, set directly underneath the top, was slightly arched on the lower edge. (See Plate 1.) Except in an occasional shop, fireplaces were not built in Shaker houses, and hence the settle was practically unknown.

PLATE 6

Ironing-room, with table and chairs

THE ironing tables used at the Enfield (Connecticut) community were of the X-trestle type. The two-piece pine top of the example in Plate 6 is solid but not heavy. Rectangular stretchers are tenoned into hardwood legs, which in turn are mortised and tenoned into cross braces set on end directly beneath the top. Every joint is doweled and the top secured by large wooden pins. Dimensions: 57 inches by 34 inches by 27 inches. Small tables of this type were used in kitchens, storerooms and printing shops; and large X-trestles were made at Harvard, Alfred, Canterbury, New Lebanon and other societies for shop service and such industries as canning and apple-sorting.

Chairs of the type shown in Plate 6 were used at counters, desks and laundry tables at New Lebanon. The one at the left is the earlier of the two. The seat of the one-slat chair is $22\frac{1}{2}$ inches from the floor; distance from top of slat to floor, $32\frac{1}{2}$ inches; width of seat, front, 19 inches; width of seat, rear, $14\frac{1}{2}$ inches. The back posts of the three-slat chair curve slightly backward and terminate in the sharply defined acorn typical of mid-century craftsmanship. The seat is 19 inches from the floor; distance from top of upper slat to floor, $40\frac{1}{4}$ inches; width of seat, front, 18 inches; width of seat, rear, 14 inches.

The towel rack has an upper rail by which it can be suspended from the wall-pegs. The flatiron rests on a wide iron band. The ironing cloth is Shaker-woven and dyed.

In the category of trestle tables belong those pieces, composed of removable board tops set on three- or four-legged horses, which were made by several families for laundry, dairy or workshop use. A fine example of this type, which also memorializes the part played by Shaker children in the daily routine, is a New Lebanon ironing table whose top, supported by two three-legged horses, is a long pine frame enclosing six small, equisized drawers. Each young Shakeress had her own place at the board, her own drawer for the finished work. In a shallow drawer, underslung at one end, were kept the holders for the irons. Ironing was an important occupation in a sect devoted to spotlessness and order. Each sister and child had to take her "tour" or turn at the laundry. The work placed such demands on these groups that the holy laws issued the warning: "Sisters may not go to ironing until they can see without a candle in the room."

Many special kinds of chairs, besides the

low dining seats, were constructed for domestic use: high-seated ones with one, two or three slats, for service at tailoring counters, shop-desks, looms or laundry tables; high and low swivel chairs, for use at school or shop-desks, or in certain industrial occupations; children's side chairs and rockers; armchairs without rockers; invalids' chairs; extra-width chairs; and side chairs and armchairs of a simplified banister type. Invalids' chairs had two slats, arms terminating in an abbreviated roll, and a cabinet under a broad seat. In another category are the cripples' walking frames or "crutchchairs," an enlarged chair base or stool frame open at one side and provided with padded grips for the hands. Footrests similar to those on babies' high chairs were sometimes added to rockers for the convenience of the feeble or aged members. In one community, the height of chair backs could be increased by an ingenious two-slat fixture which was applied to the upper slat.

PLATE 7
Ministry sisters' room. Stretcher-base table, rocking chairs and mirror.

Tables of the stretcher-base or "tavern" type were rarities of Shaker craftsmanship. The example in Plate 7, from the Second family, New Lebanon, has slightly raked legs and a drop-leaf top. The leaves are supported by butterfly-wing brackets, the inside edges of which are shaped into terminal pins which fit at the lower end into wooden fixtures and at the upper end into wrought-iron loops attached to the frame or skirting. A drawer with the large dovetailing representative of the earliest joining, extends the entire length of the frame. The top, with the leaves down, measures 40 inches by 11½ inches; with the leaves up,

40 inches by 30 inches. Height: 28 inches. Top, skirt and drawer are cherry; legs, birch.

The tape-seat rocking chairs in Plate 7 are identical, and were made on order at New Lebanon (about 1850) for the two ministry sisters in the Hancock-Tyringham-Enfield bishopric. The backs are only 12 inches wide. The legs on the stool at the left are turned like certain table-legs.

PLATE 8
Sisters' gathering or common room. Drop-leaf tables, chairs and stove.

The drop-leaf table at the left, made at Hancock about 1820, has two long, shallow, lipped drawers only 2½ inches in depth. The leaf is supported by a wrought, crane-like fixture set into rivets in the back skirt, and kept from striking the frame by a small peg. The measurements of the leg may be taken as typical of many stands. Starting at the top with a blocking 1⅝ inches square, it is altered, just beneath the junction with the frame, to a turned post whose diameter almost imperceptibly decreases from 1½ to 1⅛ inches. The dimensions of this stand, or table: 35½ inches by 15½ inches by 28 inches. The leaf is 9 inches wide. Wood: cherry.

The drop-leaf table with end drawer, made at Hancock between 1815 and 1825, measures 34¼ inches by 14½ inches by 26¾ inches with the leaves down. With the leaves up, the top is widened by 16 inches. Wood: cherry and maple.

The armchair is wider than those pictured in Plate 7, and has broader, flatter mushrooms. The sewing rocker belongs to an early period in the chair industry. It is characteristically low, the seat sloping from 14 inches above the floor in front to 13 inches in back. The front and back width of the seat are 18½ inches and 14½ inches, and the height of the chair (to top of upper slat), 34½ inches. Both chairs are from New Lebanon.

The stove is an early New Lebanon product. The steel shovel and tongs came from Hancock.

Drop-leaf tables. Tables with one or two drop-leaves were somewhat later than those with one-piece tops, but were probably being made in nearly all the eastern societies by 1815 or 1820. The principle of economy involved in such pieces appealed to the Shaker mind, and we find them used in kitchens, pantries, dairies, dining halls, retiring-rooms and nurse-shops or infirmaries. When employed as side tables in the dining room, as utility kitchen pieces, or as sisters' workroom tables, they sometimes attained a length of ten feet or more.

At the other extreme were drop-leaf tables or stands measuring little over two feet in length. (Plate 20.) The leaves on such pieces are variously supported: by one or two wooden strips pulled out by leather thongs or tiny wooden knobs from a single or double casing built into the frame; by single, hinged strips set into a slot at the top of the skirt; by the butterfly-wing brace already described; or rarely, by a gate-leg hinged by a finger-joint to the frame.

In the drop-leaf table the Shaker-turned leg achieved its most satisfying expression. At Hancock, where some of the finest examples were made, the turning of the leg surmounted by a delicate upper collar, the narrow leaves (in some cases only six inches wide), and the relatively broad top disclose on occasion the possible influence of the Sheraton school—as do the collared feet of certain Alfred stands and tables. (Plate 9.) But the taper of the typical leg is not a marked one, and in some cases the diameter remains constant. The square-tapered leg also assumed delicate lines, which, had they been inlaid, would likewise have suggested relationship with the English styles which affected American cabinetwork after the Revolution.

PLATE 9
Maine Shaker craftsmanship.
Tables and chair.

THE low splay-legged table was used in the washhouse at New Gloucester or Sabbathday Lake, Maine. It is barely two feet high, the skirt itself measuring eight inches in depth. The "bread-board" pine top (38⅛ inches by 22¼ inches) overlaps the frame 7¾ inches at each end. Skirt and legs are maple.

The oval-top table was one of several used in a sisters' shop at Alfred. The top is pine; the rest, birch. Dimensions: 30 inches by 22¾ inches by 26¾ inches.

The chair, made at New Gloucester, has the Maine characteristic of slightly shaped rungs. Heights: from top of upper slat to floor, 36½ inches; from front of seat to floor, 13½ inches; from back of seat to floor, 13 inches. It is hung on the pegboard in the Shaker manner.

The mortars and pestles were made for the medicinal herb industry at New Gloucester.

Small tables. In the class of small four-legged tables with "bread-board" or oval tops belong some of the most charming and precisely styled pieces of Shaker furniture. The characteristic leg was a turned rod, minus feet; but in certain communities, Harvard and New Lebanon for example, variations of the button foot were acceptable, and two examples of the so-called Dutch foot have been found at the latter settlement. Many four-legged tables, some approaching the dimensions of a stand, were used in the dairy, where they were sometimes called cheese-tables. Rim-top tables, usually supplied with front or end drawers, were part of the equipment of the numerous sewing shops, and in this study are classified as sewing stands. In the Maine and eastern Massachusetts communities, maple and pine tip tables were made for the sisters' shops and retiring-rooms.

PLATE 10

Kitchen table and bench

BREAD-CUTTING tables were laborsaving devices used in most Shaker dwellings. The prevalent form, exemplified by the piece in Plate 10 (from the South family, New Lebanon), had splayed legs and a heavy, almost square top, in the corner or center of which was set a long, wooden-handled knife which swung on a pivot, enabling the operator to slice quickly the homemade loaves of Indian corn, wheat or unleavened bread. In similar tables used for cutting maple sugar, the heavy top board is grooved around the edges.

PLATE 11

Shaker bake-room furnishings

NUMBERS of special-type tables were used in preparing food, canning or baking. The example in Plate 11, from the bake-room of the "North house" at New Lebanon, where it was placed soon after the building was erected in 1818, resembles a high bench to which drawers have been added. The sides or endboards are cut at the base into an arch ten inches high. A single, frontal rail joins the frame beneath the two long drawers, which are separated by a transverse brace, set on end and scrolled in the front projection. The piece, painted red, has a narrow backboard and a broad shelf below. It is 66 inches long, 22 inches wide and 28 inches high; the material is pine.

The wooden bowls and kitchen utensils are Shaker-made. The angled sides of the wooden sconce protect the candle flame from drafts.

Rarely, in the old accounts kept by the trustees of Shaker families, do we find records of the manufacture or sale of tables, or in fact, of any other furniture than chairs. Tables were a part of the "joint inheritance," made for the use of the Believers themselves. That such pieces were constructed at an early date is evidenced, however, by an entry in a New Lebanon daybook for the year 1792 which tells of a table sold for twelve shillings to Timothy Edwards of Stockbridge; one in 1806 recording the payment of one pound, fourteen shillings, to one John Shapley for a "Squair table"; and one in 1807, for one pound, eighteen shillings, to "Noah Osborn for making a table."

STANDS

PLATES 12–17

BEING the result of organic growth and necessity, and not of order by external authority, as in most institutions, the furniture of a Shaker communal dwelling has qualities of flexibility (in design and use) best evidenced, perhaps, by the amount of small furniture, especially tables and stands, distributed throughout the buildings. Variety issued from vitality. The fact was recognized that even in a communistic order, allowance should be made for individual taste as well as for personal comfort and convenience. In the Millennial Laws it was directed that "one or two stands" should be provided for the occupants of every retiring-room. Sewing shops were equipped with stands for the use of one or two individuals. Weave-rooms, seed-shops and other industrial centers needed small pieces of cabinetwork for the scientific prosecution of occupations. Wash-stands symbolized the importance and religious significance of cleanliness. The diversity of small furniture correlated with the complexity of Shaker life.

PLATE 12
Early Shaker stands

CANDLESTANDS were being made by John Shapley and others in New Lebanon as early as 1805. The presence of a number of primitive pieces, related in design to early American peg- or stick-leg stands, predicates, however, an even earlier use.

The evolution of early candlestand design is recorded in Plate 12. In the somewhat crude example at the left, from the New Lebanon Church, the pedestal is set into a heavy, round disc raised on four stubby legs; the one-board top can be raised by the shaft in the stem to which it is attached. Height, 24½ inches; top, 12¾ inches by 18 inches.

The next stand has a rimmed top, a drawer and delicate rod feet. It is 25 inches high, with a top measuring 12⅜ inches by 18⅜ inches.

Peg-leg stands with drawers were not adjustable in height. The stand in the center differs from the preceding example, however, in its wide top with cleated ends and in the collar turning which strengthens the base of the post. The bottom of the drawer is nailed on, not inserted into grooves as in the case of later stands. Height, 24 inches; top, 16 inches by 24½ inches.

Comparison of the adjustable-top stand, second from the right in Plate 12, with the crude example at the left indicates the trend toward refinement of line. The feet are widely raked and delicately turned, and the slimness and simplicity of the pedestal anticipate later conventions in candlestand design. A threaded peg in the post fastens the top at a given height. A single screw holds the top to the shaft. Top: 12½ inches by 19½ inches. Height, with top down: 24 inches.

The stand at the right is a transition piece. Its style is comparable to the second one in the group, but it has assumed the curved, molded feet of the typical Shaker light- or lampstand. Not more than twenty years, however, separate this example from the earliest stands made in the community.

The tops, casings and drawers of these pieces were usually made of pine; the pedestals and feet, of maple or some other hard wood. All are from the New Lebanon Church family.

The candle sconce is pine wood, stained an orange brown.

Tradition holds that the "peg-legs" were used beside looms or as accessories for sorting seeds, but there is no confirming evidence. From stick-leg stands evolved candle-, lamp- and bookstands with rimmed or end-cleated tops and single- or double-curved (snake) feet.

PLATE 13
"Round stand," with side chairs

THE "round stands" used in almost every Shaker retiring-room represent the final stage of evolution in candlestand design.

The typical piece is cherry, with a round top, a slender shaft expanding downward in a straight line or gentle curve, and legs cut into a convex or a double arc. In the most common examples, the line from the top of the pedestal to the foot is unbroken.

Plate 13 shows a delicate variant made at the Second family in New Lebanon. The stem is like a banister rail, increasing in diameter from $1\frac{1}{8}$ inches at the top to 2 inches at the bottom. The top ($15\frac{3}{4}$ inches in diameter) is only $\frac{1}{2}$ inch thick; the legs, $\frac{5}{8}$ of an inch. A circular disc replaces the usual cross brace under the top. The stand is $25\frac{1}{4}$ inches high.

The chairs, which came from the Enfield, New Hampshire community, weigh less than five pounds each. Cane seats were uncommon, except at this colony. Chair finials of the type shown are also characteristic of Canterbury and Maine chairs—evidence of a correspondence in the crafts of the northern New England Shaker societies. The slope of the chair seats is almost imperceptible: they are $15\frac{1}{2}$ inches from the floor in front, and 15 inches at the back. The height to the top of the upper slat is $37\frac{3}{4}$ inches.

The small, pine, wall cupboard (from the North family, New Lebanon) is a typical convenience of the sisters' shops.

PLATE 14
Workstand, with brethren's rocker and pipe-rack

TRIPOD workstands with spacious tops were uncommon items of Shaker craftsmanship. The piece in Plate 14 is pine and maple, painted dark red. The cleated top, 20 inches by $28\frac{3}{4}$ inches; height of stand, $25\frac{1}{2}$ inches. Church family or First Order, New Lebanon.

Brethren's chairs were larger and of sturdier construction than those made for the sisters. In this one (from Hancock) the seat (21 inches wide in front and $15\frac{3}{4}$ inches in back) slants from a point $14\frac{1}{2}$ inches to one 13 inches above the floor. Height to top of upper slat, 42 inches. Stained an old red.

The pipe-rack was found at Niskeyuna or Watervliet, the center of the Shaker pipe-making industry. It is of pine, stained a warm brown, with a tin tray at the base in which to rest the bowls. The long willow stems were inserted in the loops formed by a band of tin and interlocking wire fastened along a cut-out wooden strip. It could be hung on a peg. Dimensions: $11\frac{1}{2}$ inches by $13\frac{3}{4}$ inches.

Pipes with red or white clay bowls and wooden stems were made and sold at New Lebanon and Watervliet as early as 1808. The use of tobacco was prohibited in spirit messages received during the inspirational period, 1837–1847, and the industry waned about this time. That indulgence intermittently continued, however, is evidenced by the following quaint "Obituary" appearing in the *Shaker Manifesto* for 1873:

"On Tuesday, Feb. 20th, 1873, Died by the power of truth and for the cause of human Redemption, at the Young Believers' Order, Mount Lebanon, in much beloved Brethren, the Tobacco Chewing Habit, aged respectively, In D. S. 51 years' duration [etc., etc.],

"No funeral ceremonies, no monument, no graveyard; but an honorable Record thereof in the Court above."

PLATE 15
Sewing stands and chairs

THE Shaker ideas of community and convenience are expressed in the sewing stands which permitted two sisters to coöperate on a given task. These pieces had square tops, which made possible the addition of two narrow, underslung drawers, one on each side of the post. A mild compromise with principle is recorded in the simply scalloped corners of occasional top boards, or in a bit of "excess" turning on the pedestal. The drawers slide on cleats and can be pulled from either side. The variant at the right of the picture has an exposed central drawer passing freely through a narrow dovetailed frame fixed on end to the top of the pedestal. A thin, forged-iron plate, extending a half-inch or so along the base of the leg to allow for the insertion of an extra screw, was used at the base of the posts of all tripod stands to keep the legs from spreading. The wood is usually maple, though the piece at the right in Plate 15 has a pine drawer.

Dimensions of tops, and heights, left to right: 20¾ inches by 17¾ inches, 25¾ inches; 19 inches by 16¾ inches, 23⅝ inches; 21 inches by 17½ inches, 25¾ inches.

The sewing chairs made at New Lebanon during the third quarter of the nineteenth century have comparatively long rockers and tape seats. Curly maple legs and button feet distinguish the Hancock cricket. The rug is 54 inches wide.

PLATE 16
"Round stand," with early rocking chairs and clock

Scores of stands such as the one shown were constructed for brethren's and sisters' retiring-rooms. The usual height was 25 inches; the usual wood, cherry.

The four-slat rocker, made in 1801 at New Lebanon, illustrates a stage in the evolution of armchair design. The arms are crudely shaped, but the plainly turned posts, the elongated finials harmoniously continuing the line of the back posts, and the narrow, four-slat back, all forecast the typical rocker style. Its seat is 20 inches wide at the front and 15 inches at the back. Distance from floor to top of upper slat, 33¼ inches; to seat, 15 inches. The three-slat rocker is a Hancock variant, with rod-like arms entering front posts turned in one piece.

On the floor is a wooden "spit-box." During the first half of the last century these boxes, filled with sawdust or shavings, were in common use in brethren's shops and retiring-rooms. They were also sold to the world.

The clock is described on pages 111-112.

PLATE 17
Four-legged sewing stand or table. Small built-in pine cupboard with drawers.

This rimmed-top sewing stand, from the New Lebanon Church, has shallow end drawers and a deeper drawer in front and slightly below—a disposition which economizes every square inch of space in a small piece. Delicate legs taper from an inch and a quarter square to three quarters of an inch at the foot. The dimensions are 29 inches by 18 inches by 25 inches. Woods: butternut and cherry. More common but related types have one or two long drawers in front or at the ends. The view is in a third-loft room of the "Second House" at the North family, New Lebanon, built in 1818.

The Shaker phrase, "Variety in harmony is the desideratum," is peculiarly applicable to four-legged stands.

CASE-FURNITURE

PLATES 18–21. Chests, Cases of Drawers and Wood-Boxes
PLATES 22–27. Cupboard-Chests and Cupboards
PLATE 28. Sideboard
PLATES 29–30. Counters

From the time of Mother Ann to the present, proverbial attention has been paid by the Shakers to the "care and management of temporal things." The founder of the sect instructed her followers to "observe good economy; to use the things of this world as not abusing them; to be prudent and saving, and let nothing be lost or wasted through carelessness or neglect."* The Believers followed such precepts as part of the gospel. Domestic order and neatness were the individual responsibility of every occupant of a communal dwelling.

Order necessitated the construction of great numbers of chests, cases of drawers, cupboards and sets of built-in drawers. When not actually in use, all clothing, bedclothes and other textiles, tools, household utensils and accessories of many kinds were neatly put away from sight, and from dust and dirt. Coverlets, sheets and towels were marked with the name of the family, and stored in special presses. Clothes, inconspicuously initialed, were laid away in drawers or chests, or hung in the "public cupboard" on homemade hangers, also inscribed (or labeled) with the user's name or initials. Workbenches, cabinets and cupboards provided repositories for the tools and

materials used in the shops. Counters, liberally supplied with drawers, were permanent fixtures in the tailoring-rooms, offices and laundries. Built into the interior structure of the Church family dwelling at Enfield, New Hampshire, were eight hundred and sixty drawers, an average of about nine to every member who dwelt there in the middle of the last century.

Case-furniture was undoubtedly rare in the Shaker communities before 1800, though "close" chests were being made at New Lebanon in 1790, and it is probable that lift-top or blanket-chests, often supplied with one, two or even three drawers, were not uncommon at that time. Cases of drawers, equipped in one type with cupboards, made their appearance in the first decade of the nineteenth century. Both the blanket-chest and the case of drawers underwent certain modifications in style, but like the Shaker chairs maintained a specific character and purity up to the time of the Civil War.

The Shaker "six-board chest" without feet boasts little priority over those lift-top forms with molded or bracket feet. Drawerless chests in both styles were made in every community, sharing a common early origin with three-slat side chairs, benches, trestle tables, peg-leg stands and tables with one-

*Testimonies of the life, character, revelations and doctrines of our ever blessed mother Ann Lee, p. 263.

piece tops. The material was white pine, painted a dark, flat red. The lids, made of one board, were usually edged with a thumbnail molding and hinged on staples or wrought straps. In the finer pieces the frame was joined by large dovetails, which also secured the corners of the base brackets. The feet were shaped into an ogee curve or a simple arc; sometimes they were applied to the frame as part of the base molding, and sometimes cut out of the frame itself, as in the simpler six-board chests. On the earliest examples the backboard is riven or cleaved, as were the blocks set inside the rear feet to supply strength. Within the chest there is usually a stationary or movable till, sometimes one at each end, with lids hinged to the chest frame and often with a drawer just below. An occasional example has wrought handles clinched into the ends through an oval plate. Cast handles were later additions.

PLATE 18

Chests and chairs for children

Two small chests from Hancock. Construction and relative proportions are those of the larger storage chests, but the pieces have distinctive character. In the smaller one, the lid of the till has a thumbnail molding corresponding to that of the chest lid. The cleats are beveled along the side, and at the front and back; staple-hinges, a dovetailed frame, and small blocks inside the base brackets testify to a relationship with the conventional chests. The smaller piece, made of birch, measures 16 inches by 7 inches by $9\frac{5}{8}$ inches. The larger chest is pine; dimensions, 25 inches by 12 inches by 16 inches.

The side chair in Plate 18, which is older than the rocker, is equipped with the ball-and-socket feet. Tradition ascribes it to the Canaan workshop of Gilbert Avery. The rocker is from the New Lebanon community. Its seat is $15\frac{1}{4}$ inches wide in front, and 12 inches in back. Height: to front of seat, $11\frac{5}{8}$ inches; to back of seat, $10\frac{1}{4}$ inches; to top of upper slat, $24\frac{1}{2}$ inches.

The presence of locks on the two chests in Plate 18 is somewhat exceptional—as it was in all case-furniture. In the "Orders Rules and Counsels for the People of God" (February 18, 1841), it was directed that "ye shall not lock, nor fasten by secret means, nor cause it to be done, any cupboard, draw, chest, or writing box belonging to any individual." The Millennial Laws also required that "no private possession should be kept under lock and key security, without liberty from the Elders," adding that "it is desirable to have all so trustworthy that locks and keys will be needless." To have locks "in the dwelling house of the saints" was to silently indict the saintliness of its occupants. In the few pieces of furniture where locks are found, the escutcheons are made of horn, bone or ivory.

PLATE 19

Blanket- or storage chests

THE one-drawer chest made by Gilbert Avery at the Canaan (New York) Upper family (a branch of the North family, New Lebanon) is inscribed on the back in burned letters: "Made April, 1837. Canaan." It is painted red. Escutcheons are bone. Dimensions: 41 inches by 18 inches by $27\frac{1}{2}$ inches. The style of the two-drawer chest, from the South family, was duplicated in other New Lebanon families, notably the North and Church. They were stained red, orange or yellow. Both chests are pine. The picture was taken in the attic of the South family dwelling.

In colonial New York and New England, the plain box or lift-top chest had acquired one or two drawers at an early period. Models of the so-called blanket-chests thus already existed, and the earliest Shaker pieces, though devoid of carving or painted decoration, might readily be taken for colonial chests. But when the inevitable transition to an even simpler design took place, the Shaker chests assumed a distinctive style. Of sheer simplicity were those made at the North and Church families in New Lebanon. These typical pieces had one or two flush, bevel-edged drawers, and bracket feet cut so as to form an angle with the frame ranging from 103 to 108 degrees. The applied bracket foot, formed into an ogee or simple convex curve, was varied by feet cut from the frame boards. At the base of the sides we find the conventional round or Gothic arch which was a feature of most Shaker benches.

PLATE 20
Small case of drawers and drop-leaf table

SMALL cases of drawers were made for the Children's Order or for special occupational uses. The low, deep chest in Plate 20 was the work of Abner Alley of the Enfield (Connecticut) Shakers in 1849. It is 24 inches by 18⅜ inches by 27½ inches. Wood: butternut. Many small cabinets or cases were used for tools, seeds or packages of herbs.

The table, made at the New Lebanon Church, served a special need or was intended for the Children's Order. Wood: cherry. The top (with leaves down) is 27 inches by 12 inches, and with leaves up, 15 inches wider. The piece is 26 inches high.

A wooden foot warmer hangs on the peg.

The picture shows an attic storage room of the large brick dwelling at the Hancock Church, built in 1830.

PLATE 21
Wood-box and washstand

THE washstand (from the South family, New Lebanon) also serves as a small case of drawers. A small towel-drying rack is affixed to the top of the wood-box, which came from the nurse-shop or infirmary at the New Lebanon Church. The washstand is painted red. Dimensions: 46 inches by 22½ inches by 30 inches (exclusive of back- and sideboards). The wood-box measures 30½ inches by 12½ inches by 57 inches (to top of rack). The small wall-box is neatly dovetailed. All pieces, pine.

Large boxes, with lidded covers and tin or wooden fixtures on the side for holding shovels and tongs, were used in shops, halls and retiring-rooms to hold fuel for the small wood-burning stoves. Hancock examples were 24 inches high, 25 inches wide and 16 inches deep, with a narrow, quarter-round base molding and a partition inside to separate the kindlings from the wood. Boards with rounded ends were placed vertically inside the box so that the wood could be piled high—an example of the Shaker instinct for economy. The frame was dovetailed and painted a pale chrome yellow. Hatboxes were made with similar proportions, and with four long pegs inside on which to hang the brethren's felt, "caster" or colt's fur hats. Delicately constructed, handled carriers called chip-boxes, rectangular in shape, were employed in many communities for fetching kindlings from the woodhouse. (See Plate 21.)

More commodious wood-boxes, often painted red, held material for the kitchen stoves or arches. Shops and schoolrooms were at times similarly equipped, and spacious receptacles were needed for the laundry stoves. The front boards were high enough to support a plentiful supply of wood and low enough to allow its being conveniently reached. Wood-boxes had a drawer at the top or base for kindling. A fine example from the North family in New Lebanon had bracket feet and a paneled door. Another, from Canterbury, is like a high schoolmaster's desk, with its sloping lid giving access to a deep well, its drawer at the base for kindling, and the arched cutout at the base of the boards forming the sides. Large wood-boxes at this community were "built into the walls like closets, with trap doors to them close by the stoves, so that no wood, splinters or dirt is seen."*

PLATE 22

High cupboard-chest and step-stool

PINE case of drawers with cupboard top, typical of the work of Elder Amos Stewart of the New Lebanon Church. Dated "December, 1830." It is 72 inches high, 42 inches wide and 18¼ inches deep.

Pine stools called "two-steppers," "three-steppers" and "four-steppers" rendered accessible the top drawers of the high Shaker cases or built-in drawers. From the top of some of these small stepladders projected an upright handle or steadying rod. The stool in Plate 22 is 25¼ inches high, 15¾ inches long and 11½ inches wide at the base. The top step is 6 inches wide.

Cupboard-chests and large chests of drawers. The Shaker cupboard-chest, combining the advantages of drawers and cupboard space, was a more distinct, and in certain com-

munities at least, a more common type of furniture than the frame entirely occupied by drawers. Cases with upper or lower cupboards were built into the wall structure of the earliest shops and dwellings,† and their manufacture as a movable piece probably antedates by a considerable period the year 1819, the date inscribed on the earliest marked example. The arrangement of drawers and the relationship between the drawers and the cupboards conform to no particular pattern. One cupboard may surmount another at the top; a single cupboard may be built at the bottom; or single or double cupboards may be constructed at both the top and bottom of the frame, with drawers between. In most pieces, however, the single or double cupboard was placed at the top. Such chests were often made without feet, especially those in which the cupboard was constructed at the base of the frame. The footless cupboard-chests were usually provided with a base molding.

Against the simple, white-plastered walls of a Shaker room these cupboards assumed a peculiar architectural dignity. Reaching a normal height of six or seven feet, they contained on occasions as many as twelve drawers, those at the top and the bottom sometimes being paired. The cupboard doors usually had flat, sunken panels surrounded by a beveled or sharply edged frame. The fielded panel appears more frequently on early built-in cupboards and movable shop types. On one New Lebanon example, three vertical bands of fielded paneling border the two doors. H-hinges were used on some of the first high chests, but a more typical feature was the long, wrought pin screwed into the edge of the

---

*Pomeroy, M. M. *Visit to the Shakers*, p. 8.

†Built-in drawers and cupboards were constructed in duplicate in certain dwellings, so that they could be used from either one of two adjoining rooms.

door, which served as an automatic catch to hold it closed. Cupboard interiors were sometimes shelved across or on the side. Probably to economize space, the short bracket feet seldom raised the chest over 2½ to 3 inches above the floor. The wood was invariably pine, varnished in the later examples, thinly stained or painted red or yellow in those of greater age.

High chests made up entirely of drawers arranged in a single or double row and graduated in size, were typical of all the eastern communities. The feet were of the non-projecting, curved or angled bracket type, cut from or joined to the frame. Blocks tapered at the base and set inside of these brackets helped to support the great weight of the piece.

Wooden drawer-knobs, sparingly used in eighteenth- and nineteenth-century American cabinetwork, materially aid in giving case-furniture a distinct character. In the Shaker equivalent of the highboy and chest-on-chest, small and large drawers (sometimes twelve or more) are arranged in many patterns. The completed unit is a study in symmetry. The breakup of the great frontal surface into the oblongs of drawers, the lines of small, neatly turned knobs, and the light finish revealing the grain of the pine, protect such chests and cupboards from an appearance of bulkiness and imbue them with the same unpretentious gracefulness of smaller cases. The earliest pieces were painted red. Late chests were treated with a red or yellow ochre wash, and later still with varnish.

PLATE 23

High pine case with base cupboard

FROM North family shop, New Lebanon. It is 77¼ inches high, 29 inches wide and only 11⅝ inches deep. Pipe-box from Niskeyuna.

PLATE 24

"Weave-chest" or sill cupboard, with accessories

THE cupboard-chest in Plate 24, of beautifully grained pine, was found in a weave-room in the washhouse of the New Lebanon Church family. It is 73¼ inches high, 31½ inches wide, 13 inches deep above the sill, and 18 inches deep below the sill. Note the narrowness of the cupboard door. Its original color was red. The reel at the left is from New Lebanon, its neighbor from Hancock, and the one at the right from Enfield in Connecticut. Some of the spools on the hanging scarn retain their Shaker-spun yarns.

The sill cupboards were a not uncommon form of the Shaker cupboard-chest. In some, the section below the sill was occupied by a cupboard, sometimes surmounted by one or two drawers; in others, the upper section was enclosed by narrow doors set with small glass panes. Small "pan" or "spider" cupboards were used at Hancock in cellars and pantries. At Niskeyuna, interesting adaptations exist of the rare colonial livery cupboards.

PLATE 25

Cellar cupboard and bench

PINE cupboard found in the subcellar of the First Order dwelling, Church family, New Lebanon. A very early example of Shaker workmanship. Painted a deep red, it may have been used in a shop. Dimensions: 75½ inches high (36 inches from sill to floor and 39½ inches from sill to top); 19¾ inches wide; 17 inches deep (below sill); and 11 inches deep (above sill).

Benches for farm, shop, storeroom or cellar use, with heavy tops and turned or planed leg-posts, ranged in size from great butchering tables to the low floor racks used to keep chests and boxes off the attic or basement floors. Wash-tubs and keelers in the laundry; wash-tubs, milk pans, "calf" pails and cheeses in the dairy; "black kettles," chopping or mixing bowls, vegetable boxes and flour and sugar pails in the bake-shop; and applesauce buckets, grain and seed pails, baskets, boxes, tools and a hundred other objects in the brethren's shops—all were orderly arranged on shelves and benches. The humblest of all furniture, the bench served countless basic needs in the complex domestic-industrial life of the sect. The example in Plate 25 is 29 inches by 12¾ inches by 21½ inches. The top (3¼ inches thick) is chamfered along the lower edges. Painted a deep red.

The picture shows a cellar in the Hancock Church family dwelling.

PLATE 26
Built-in drawers and cupboards

A CORNER of the meeting-room in the family dwelling of the Hancock Church, built in 1830. Woodwork: pine. The three-step stool is 25¼ inches high, 17½ inches wide, and 13¾ inches deep at the base.

PLATE 27
Built-in cupboards and drawers
in brethren's retiring-room

A ROOM in the South family dwelling, New Lebanon. Built-in drawers and cupboards were common in nurse-shops for the convenient storage of medicinal supplies. Here the woodwork is butternut.

The brethren's armed rocker, made of cherry, is unusually high, 45¼ inches to the top of the upper slat. The seat slopes from a height of 16¾ inches in front to 14¼ inches at the back, and diminishes in width from 20 inches to 15½ inches. The splint in the seat is very narrow.

The cherry and maple table is 72 inches by 26¾ inches by 27¾ inches. The top overlaps the frame 18 inches at each end. On the table is a flat-topped, two-drawer lap- or table-desk.

The two-step foot bench or sewing stool provided a natural rest for the feet, one above the other, so that when the legs were crossed, a book or needlework was elevated to a convenient height. Some were made with a lidded top and space for sewing materials. Robert Wagan manufactured a two-step "sewing-bench" and a "foot-bench" with sloping top and turned legs strengthened by two side rungs, a piece "nicely adapted for the purpose of kneeling stools." Certain types of stools resembled miniature benches; many had vertical or splayed leg-boards and a medial brace just beneath the top. The Shaker milking stool had three legs and a circular or half-circular top which sometimes was cut out to form a projecting handle. The initials of the sister by whom it was used were often painted under the top. Peg-leg stools or crickets of various designs protected the feet from the cold floors of the early Shaker dwellings.

PLATE 28
Sideboard used by Canterbury ministry

ONLY one true sideboard, as distinguished from the dining-hall side tables, serving tables or bread-cutting tables, has come within the collecting experience of the authors. This piece was in early use in the ministry's dining room at the Canterbury community. The top board, apparently of native walnut, is pinned to a frame made up of square lengths of birch securely mortised together. The stiles, turned just below the bottom rail, hold the frame about 9½ inches above the floor. The ends of the piece are inset panels of pine. Two doors, also of pine, are similarly paneled and separated by a vertical strip 4⅝ inches wide; the door rails are tongue-and-grooved into the the stiles. Hammered iron catches at the top hold the doors tightly closed. A long pine rack or shelf, built against the backboard, increases the usefulness of the piece. Into the frame (which is 4 feet, 10 inches long, 33⅛ inches high and 21 inches deep) is fitted a service slide (1 inch in thickness) with end cleats and a wider frontal strip pegged on with small dowels. On a peg at the side, similar to the ones on the doors, was hung a brush. The piece was originally painted red.

PLATE 29
Long tailoring counter

A TYPE found both at Hancock and New Lebanon. Top and drawer fronts, curly maple. Top, exclusive of leaf: 76¼ inches by 31 inches. Height 33 inches. At the right, a spool stand with drawers, small cupboard and rack for spools.

Counter and stand were made at the North family, New Lebanon, where the picture was taken. Note the ventilation holes in the baseboard. "Good ventilation," wrote Wingate in 1880, "is a constant study. Slats are placed in every window to make an opening between the two sashes, so that there shall always be an influx of atmospheric air. Small holes along the baseboard in all of the halls aid this end."

Counters. The industries of dressing cloth and making hats, mittens and clothes, for market as well as domestic consumption, date back to the first years of organized Shakerism. As early as 1789, the tailor brethren of New Lebanon were at work on coats, surtouts, vests, breeches, overalls and jackets; and soon afterward an "order" of tailoresses assumed responsibility for

the sisters' clothing. At first the cloth was cut, pieced and sewed on tables, but with the advent of more comfortable circumstances the Believers devised the convenient combination of table and chest of drawers known as a tailoring-bench, tailors' table or counter. By 1825, when the trade underwent reorganization and a degree of standardization, such pieces had become characteristic appointments of the brethren's and sisters' shops. Like many special kinds of chairs, tables and chests, and like the sewing stands described in the following section, the counter exemplifies the organic relationship of craftsmanship with home and shop industry.

Though subject to those variations which rise from locale, function and individuality of workmanship, the typical Shaker counter can nevertheless be recognized by its length and height, its substructure of equisized drawers arranged in a double or single row, and the depth of the frame and breadth of the top, in many pieces extensible by a drop-leaf at the back. Early counters were built into the recessed walls of a room, and when conceived as a separate unit, often retained the quality of a permanent fixture. As in the case of many cupboard-chests, weight and bulk made moving difficult and feet superfluous. Exceptions occurred, however, where short legs or feet were added or where small wooden rollers set into the base of the frame facilitated transference. Smaller counters, not unlike cases of drawers, suggest individual rather than communal use. Pine was the popular wood, but maple was not uncommon.

The counters' relationship with the chest of drawers on one hand, and with large tables on the other, is illustrated by many divergent pieces used in other occupations than tailoring, and in other rooms than the dressmaking shops. The height of tailoring-benches varied from 32 inches to 34 inches; and a "counter" over the latter height (some stood at least four feet from the floor) was probably used as a case of drawers for store or household service. Small counters can usually be distinguished from small chests of drawers by the frontal or lateral extension of the top and the absence of legs or top and base moldings; but sometimes the difference is not immediately apparent. Several long, low, work counters within the writers' acquaintance are provided with fine moldings, and many examples of the counter-case, seen apart from their original setting, are unclassifiable in name and particular function. Counters or cases were built along the wall in kitchens, attics and workshops, often extending the length or width of the room. A sisters' herb-shop at New Lebanon, used for filling bottles, labeling and packaging, was thus equipped; and in many a hall or "loft," the vista is of row upon row of polished drawer fronts and shining pulls. At Hancock and other societies, cloth counters with broad surfaces and a single large drawer stood on relatively high, turned legs so that the piece resembled, and probably was originally called a "table."

Store, kitchen, workshop and infirmary counters were usually longer than, and not as wide or deep, as the tailoring-benches. The first store at New Lebanon, erected in 1791, was probably equipped with these long fixed cases of drawers, for the Believers were known to have been selling goods at retail in the village late in the eighteenth century, long before the present office building (also furnished with stationary counters) was built in 1825. In these centers of trade the traditional order and cleanliness prevailed. Chairs stood

along the walls awaiting the prospective customer. Brooms and brushes and mops hung on the pegs. Baskets and a miscellaneous assortment of coopers-ware were trimly displayed on benches, or along the floor. On shelves and counters, in cupboards and drawers were arranged such smaller merchandise as pipes and pens, buttons, shoe and stock buckles, whips and braided whiplashes, wire and silk and horsehair sieves, nests of oval boxes, bolts of home-woven, home-dyed cloth, and the fine handicraft of the sisters' shops.

PLATE 30
Tailoresses' shop. Counter, chairs and looking glass.

THE small Niskeyuna counter in Plate 30 illustrates the frequent practice of paneling the sides or ends of the frame. A horizontal rail, edged with a quarter-round molding, divides the end (and in this case, also the back) into two narrow panels; the stiles and the upper and lower rails are similarly molded, the former terminating below the frame in turned legs about five inches high. The top and drawer faces of this piece, which was intended for cutting out and piecing small patterns, were made of curly maple. Stiles and rails of ungrained maple, panels of pine.

Top of counter, with leaf down, measures 45 inches by 24 inches. The leaf is $6\frac{3}{4}$ inches wide. Height of piece, 32 inches.

Chairs from Hancock. The seat of the curly maple rocker is unusually low, only $12\frac{1}{2}$ inches from the floor; it is also smaller than in most chairs of this type, $18\frac{1}{2}$ inches wide in front and $13\frac{3}{4}$ inches wide in back. The seat of the high ironing or counter chair is $24\frac{1}{2}$ inches from the floor. The top of the upper slat is 40 inches from the floor, an unusual height for this type of chair, the two slats of which are ordinarily set nearer together. The maker expended greater pains on the shaping of the feet than on the top finials.

The mirror frame (16⅜ inches by 12¼ inches) is veneered with curly maple on the front and sides, the side-strips forming a beveled edge around the frame. Made at Hancock.

Looking glasses. In the formative years of Shakerism a subtle conflict was waged between utilitarianism and worldliness. In a resurrection order, the line between what was useful and what was superfluous or sinful could not always be precisely drawn. Mirrors were first considered luxuries and instruments of vanity, instances being recorded when the followers of Ann Lee "dashed upon the floor and stamped to pieces . . . superfluous furniture, such as ornamented looking glasses, etc. . . . ear and finger rings were bitten with all the symptoms of rage, and then sold for old metal."* This was done, it seems, "to testify their abhorrence of that pride which introduced these things among mankind— and likewise as a type of the destruction of Babylon."

But the convenience of looking glasses in promoting neatness, cleanliness and uniformity slowly became recognized. In 1808, two were purchased from Albany for the Church family in New Lebanon, and several more during the first quarter of the century. The feeling against ornament still

persisted, however, and we find numbers of Chippendale-style mirrors the scrolled projections of which have been cut down so that only the inner molding remained. The allowance for retiring-rooms in 1845 was:

"One good looking glass, which ought not to exceed eighteen inches in length, and twelve in width, with a plain frame. A looking glass larger than this, ought never to be purchased by Believers. If necessary a small glass may hang in the closet, and a very small one may be kept in the public cupboard of the room."

Shaker-made looking glasses were first made soon after 1821, when the holy laws permitting their use were originally transcribed. On January 30, 1835, one was sold for 37½ cents, and on November 19, a pair for 63 cents. Typical frames consisted of four convex moldings mitered at the corners. The woods were pine, cherry, maple, curly maple and mahogany. The prescribed dimensions were closely approximated: many were exactly 12 inches by 18 inches, few if any diverging over an inch and a half from this standard. The frames (properly provided with glass) were fitted into the grooved base of a rack resembling a T-square, the vertical member of which was perforated at the top so that it could be hung on a wall-peg. A cord held the top of the frame at a convenient forward pitch. On miniature pegs at the base of the rack were suspended a comb and Shaker brushes.

Mirror and rack in Plate 7 from the South family, New Lebanon.

*Brown, Thomas. *An Account of the People called Shakers*, pp. 320–321.

SEWING STANDS
PLATES 31–34

A MORE common but no less distinctive type of Shaker furniture was the sewing stand, which in certain communities and periods assumed the additional function of a desk. An order of tailors could equip a family with the necessary outer clothing, but the hands of many sisters, young and old, were required to supply stockings and underclothes, shirts and collars; to mend clothes; to finish the cloth-and-leather gloves; to make seed-bags; to line and furnish sewing boxes; to weave the fine ash and poplar baskets; to braid palm leaf for mats and bonnets; and to make the fans, dusters, penwipers, cushions, spool stands and numerous other articles of handicraft so useful to a well-ordered communal life and so prized by the people of the world. The sewing stand—termed also a sewing table, sewing cabinet, sewing desk or workstand—served as the central implement in all this manifold activity. Used by the individual rather than the group, it often exhibited a marked individuality of design.

The typical sewing stand had small drawers encased in an upright rack or cabinet at the back, one to three larger drawers in the frame, and between these, provision for a cutting board or a broad cutting surface or sill. Such boards might be an integral part of the piece, fitted into the frame and capable of being pulled out when needed; but often they were made as separate units or parts which could be placed on the lap or on wooden slides drawn out from the sides of the frame. The feasibility of these boards as writing tablets gave use in some communes to the term "sewing desk." The setting was the sisters' shop, which might be a separate building or a room set aside for sewing and dressmaking in the communal dwelling.

PLATE 31
Sewing stands, with swivel-stools

SMALL sewing stands or sewing desks were made for children and for sisters engaged on fine projects of handicraft. The example at the right in Plate 31 dates back to the early years at Sabbathday Lake. It is $23\frac{3}{4}$ inches long by $17\frac{7}{8}$ inches deep. Frontal height, 26 inches; height at back, 32 inches. Wood, pine.

The stand by the window (painted a rich red) was made at the New Lebanon Church family. The rimmed top prevented pins, needles, small pieces of cloth, etc., from falling off a limited surface. The open tills at the top were used for tools and materials. Dimensions: length, $24\frac{1}{2}$ inches; depth, $18\frac{1}{2}$ inches; height to top of rim in front, $24\frac{3}{4}$ inches, and to top of back, $30\frac{3}{4}$ inches.

The idea of elevating the sides and back of an ordinary stand or table so that small drawers could be accommodated above the working surface, seems to have originated in the northern New England settlements; pieces with sloping sides and sometimes a frontal slide were included in the earliest furniture made at Alfred, New Gloucester, Enfield, New Hampshire and Canterbury. The pattern was apparently copied by the eastern Massachusetts communities. The Maine stands had two small upper drawers, placed side by side, and a lower tier of three or four longer ones. The former were fitted into a narrow casing which in some pieces formed the top of the stand and in others was set just below the top of a slightly rounded or arched backboard. Though the frame was often dovetailed at the top, the drawer joints were usually rabbeted. The sloping sides may have been suggested by the colonial slant-top desk. A number of smaller pieces, similarly constructed, were made in Maine especially for the girls' order. In the illustrated example, which was painted a robin's-egg blue over a yellow ground color, the cutting board was made to fit like a lid on the top long drawer, pulling out with the drawer and detachable at will.

In the New Lebanon sewing stand pictured in Plate 31, the applied rim is higher than usual and finely molded on the outer edge. On the back of the top, fitting tightly inside this rim, is a rack containing one long drawer surmounted by an open till divided into three compartments for buttons, spools or small tools. The drawer slides out on slender bearing-rails slightly angled at the end (to stop the drawer from falling out) and applied to abbreviated, sloping sides. Gracefully turned legs, braced by stretchers at the sides, support a frame accommodating a single drawer. The wood is maple and cherry.

Original products of Shaker ingenuity were the swivel chairs, also termed "revolving-stools," "revolvers," "turning-chairs" or "stool-chairs." The earliest examples were high, seat elevations ranging from twenty-eight to thirty-eight inches, and usually they were painted the dull red indicative of brethren's shop use. The seat revolved on a wooden or iron rod inserted in a cross brace at the top of the frame and pivoted in a socket in the medial-brace (or cross braces) which strengthened the high legs. These legs were shaped in the wave-like pattern of a bamboo Windsor chair leg, and were raked for stability. The back rest, if present, was almost identical with that of the Shaker cobblers' benches. (See Plate 47.)

Low swivel-stools, without backs and with Windsor-like turnings and cross stretchers, were rarely made before 1850, though such forms probably suggested the pattern of the low revolving-chairs made for household use later in the century. In one type of turning-chair the back rest, reminiscent of the Windsor comb, is composed of six or more delicate wooden spindles fitted into a curved rail, the round, maple seat rotating on a frame similar in general design to that of the high swivels. In another form the spindles (usually eight in number) may be steel wire as well as wood; a turned pedestal, gradually increasing in diameter toward the base, replaces the open frame; and the feet are two hardwood sections slightly tapered at the tips and crossed in a low arch. The seat of the stool at right (in Plate 31) is 15 inches in diameter and 19 inches from the floor; that of the stool at left, $12\frac{3}{4}$ inches in diameter and $19\frac{3}{4}$ inches from the floor.

In 1863, low swivel chairs were sold at the South family in New Lebanon for two dollars apiece, and high revolving-stools for two dollars and a half. "Desk-stools," presumably the same as the low turning-chairs, were listed in 1874 at four dollars each. In the latter part of the century, the world's people purchased such chairs for use at school-desks, sewing machines and pianos.

PLATE 32

Large sewing desk

AN unusual example of the type known as sewing desk, from the now extinct Enfield (New Hampshire) community, where it may have been used by the girls' caretaker. It is 38¾ inches long and 26⅜ inches deep (from front of writing or sewing surface). Height in front is 25⅝ inches, and in back, 35½ inches. Pine, with hardwood legs. Color, deep red.

The chair has its original leather seat. Note the small pegs under the window sill for brushes, tools, etc.

In the desk illustrated in Plate 32 the sides and back of the lower frame, which contains two tiers of two drawers each, are flat pine panels set within the stiles and cross rails. The upper part of the desk, enclosing two tiers of five small drawers each, is slightly wider and longer than the base. Gracefully sloping sides, a long slide and relatively high legs complete a piece of exceptional interest.

PLATE 33

Sewing cabinets or tables from Hancock

THE top of the five-drawer table is 37 inches by 15¾ inches, with the leaf down. The leaf adds 8½ inches to the top width. Height: 27 inches. The frame itself is 26¼ inches by 13½ inches. Mixed woods, chiefly maple. The top of the eight-drawer table is 31 inches by 22¾ inches. The frame of the cabinet is 23 inches by 16¼ inches. Height of table: 29 inches. Mixed woods.

The butternut sewing cabinets produced at Hancock are really small cases of drawers. Small, lipped drawers, provided with delicately turned knobs and arranged in many patterns, compactly occupied a low frame raised from the floor on short, squared or turned legs. In one type a drop-leaf at the back transformed the top into a more convenient working surface. In the absence of a slide, rods could sometimes be pulled out from casings at the side to hold separate lap boards. The square central drawer in one of the cabinets illustrated is provided with a device which ingeniously controls the locking of all the drawers in the piece. Small brackets, reminiscent of New Hampshire craftsmanship, were often employed to strengthen the joints where the legs met the frame. Contemporary with these Hancock "tables" were the tripod sewing stands with one or two drawers, previously described (Plate 15).

The sconce was made for two candles.

PLATE 34

Furniture unit in sisters' shop

A SEWING table from Hancock illustrating another arrangement of small drawers. Cherry, maple, butternut and pine were used in the construction of these pieces, which were said to have been made at the West family, possibly by David Terry, the family elder. On the table is an oval box with handle, commonly called a "carrier."

The sewing chair and bonnet-mold on standard came from the New Lebanon Church. The mold or form, around which the woven straw or palm leaf was shaped in making a bonnet of this size, is in three sections. It may be placed at a convenient height or position by inserting the rod in a hole bored in the top of the upright, or in holes bored slantwise near the top of the pedestal.

WRITING-DESKS

PLATES 35–38

AMONG the unprinted regulations of the early Shaker sect were two orders, restrictive in character, which reveal that written communication was tolerated though not encouraged by the Lead:

"IT is contrary to order to write a letter without retaining a copy."

"It is contrary to order to receive or write a letter without the Elders' perusal of it."*

"Portable writing desks" were forbidden in the Orders, Rules and Counsels for the People of God (1841), which also prohibited brethren and sisters from writing for or "to each other without the approbation of the Elders . . . No writing is to go out of, nor come into the family without the knowledge of the Elders." Again, in the Millennial Laws of 1845, writing-desks were classed as "superfluities," the order reading that they "may not be used by common members, only by permission of the Elders." All such regulations were part of the program to keep the worldly separate from the redeemed. Especially in the Church orders of each society was unworldliness carried to its logical extremes, and the need for desks in the early Shaker communities was therefore limited. Desks were infrequently made and conformed to no special pattern.

For the convenient pursuance of official duties, however, a few such pieces were fashioned for the elders and trustees or deacons of every colony. It was

* Haskett, William J. *Shakerism Unmasked*, p. 178.

the responsibility of the "heads of the family" to keep a "journal of meetings and other spiritual things." The Laws further state:

"A JOURNAL of all the work done and proceedings of a temporal nature in the family, may be kept by order of the Deacons and Deaconesses, or Caretakers—

"Those appointed to transact business of a temporal nature, should keep all their accounts booked down, regular and exact."

Hundreds of books, pamphlets, tracts and broadsides were written by leaders in the society, and a voluminous manuscript literature testifies to frequent expression, even on the part of the common members. "Ye may make plain bound Books [the Laws conceded] for writing hymns, anthems, journals, accounts, etc." Seedsmen, herbalists and botanists, tanners, gardeners, mechanics, basketmakers, weavers and dyers kept records for "the use and convenience" of their departments. Diaries of daily events were common, and the copying of hymns and religious "testimonies" was at all times encouraged.

Desks were also needed when the Shaker schools reached the stage of dissatisfaction with the ill-contrived early equipment. The earliest school-desks were crude affairs, boards nailed around four square posts, with sloping tops sectioned off for two or three pupils. In 1801, when Hannah Bronson was appointed to teach the children of the Be-

lievers at Canterbury, she was "ac-
comodated with a room in the blacksmith shop." In 1805 she

"kept school on the driving floor of the
barn. As the place was destitute of furniture, the children were seated on the floor,
except those who were fortunate enough to
find a box or a block of wood . . . . Ink was
too expensive to be bought, and what little
was used was made from the berries found
in the pastures." (Canterbury MS.)

At Lebanon, improved educational
advantages were introduced in 1808,
though the school at the Church order
was kept intermittently until 1815.* All
children entering the society with their
parents, or under indenture agreements
between their guardians and the elders,
were taught the common branches. In
1817, the Lancasterian system was adopted at the parent society, with a three-
months' summer session for the boys,
and a similar period in the winter for
the girls; and in 1821, Seth Youngs
Wells of Niskeyuna, a former schoolmaster, was appointed "superintendent
of Believers' literature and schools" in
the first bishopric, extending his work
later to other societies. Long before a
separate school was erected at New
Lebanon (1839), various systems had
become organized, subject to town laws,
and carefully executed pieces of furniture had replaced the early makeshift
desks.

* The earliest pronouncement on the government and
education of Shaker children is found in Chapter III,
Part II of *A Summary View of the Millennial Church*, by
Calvin Green and Seth Y. Wells, written at New Lebanon and published in Albany in 1823.

PLATE 35
Corner of early Shaker schoolroom.
Desk, bench and hanging rack.

THE bench accompanied the desk when
found. The hanging bookrack (59 inches
long) was formerly used in a schoolroom
at the North family. By the "clock" device,
children at the Watervliet settlement were
initiated into the mysteries of telling time.
It is dated 1870.

The desk (from the New Lebanon Church)
probably dates back to the Lancasterian
period, when monitors or selected pupils
were first taught the lesson by the precep-
tor and then instructed the group to which
they were assigned; the economies of such
a method might well have appealed to the
Shakers. On each side of this piece are three
tablets which are held open at a convenient
slant by brackets set flush with the sides of
the frame. Under each tablet or lid is a well
for books and papers, and a long till for pencils and pens sectioned off at one end for an
inkstand. The lids close up, being held secure by small brass catches, allowing the
desk to be used as a level-surfaced table.
The legs are tenoned into the skirt on the
extreme corners. Dimensions: 70 inches by
26 inches by $27\frac{1}{4}$ inches. Wood, cherry.

PLATE 36
High pine desk used by trustees

AN uncorroborated story assigns this desk
to the two trustees or deacons of the Second
order of the Church family, New Lebanon.
The order, established in 1814, became
known as the Center family in the late 1870's.
Each deacon was said to have had his own
writing tablet, set of drawers, pigeonholes
and shelves.

Certainly the design is dual, if not the
use. The two lids let down on a narrow sill

which separates a double row of drawers below from the rows of shelves above. The upper section of the desk is divided into two parts, one enclosed by doors and the other by the closed lids. The writing tablets and doors have the typical, slightly depressed paneling of Shaker cabinetwork. The writing surface was achieved by mortising thin boards into a bordering frame on the inner sides of the lids. Two small drawers below a row of pigeonholes are cut at the sides so that when pulled out, they can be tilted above the edges of the tablet, which otherwise would restrict the operation. The piece is pine, stained a rose-brown color.

In spite of its size and height (84¾ inches), the desk is well proportioned and graceful in appearance. The width is 48 inches, the depth (above sill), 10⅞ inches, and the depth (below sill), 16½ inches.

Hanging on a peg is a brother's felt hat. A Shaker-made cane stands in the corner of the room.

Large secretaries in native woods, usually with angular or curved bracket-feet, a simple top-molding and a short writing tablet supported by a sill, were made at Watervliet, New Lebanon, Hancock, Harvard and probably at other communities.

PLATE 37
Deaconess' desk

THIS desk, similar to ones found at Enfield and possibly made at the Connecticut society, was used for a long time in the retiring-room of a Church family deaconess at Hancock. Most of the Enfield pieces (used in schoolrooms) lack the molding at the base of the desk-box. Curly maple was often used in the construction. Here the pedestal and feet are curly maple, and the top, pine. The desk is 24½ inches long, 17¾ inches

deep, 24 inches high in front, and 28½ inches high in back.

The New Lebanon side chair, made entirely of curly maple and stained red, is equipped with the metallic ball-and-socket device patented in 1852. The composition ball is attached to a brass collar which fits over the base of the leg-post. The cane seat is 16¾ inches from the floor, a little over the average height for side chairs.

On the wall is an early railroad map (from a Shaker school) of New England and eastern New York, on which may be located the sites of all the communities of concern to us in the present study. Leather-bound Shaker books are arranged on a simple bookrack from the South family at New Lebanon.

Among the unique Shaker desks discovered by the authors may be mentioned: (1) one with sloping front and three drawers; (2) a bureau or "butler's" desk; (3) a slant-top cabinet inserted in an upright post (set on trestle feet) and held at the height desired by pegs inserted in this post; and (4) a drop-leaf table one of whose leaves can be set at a convenient pitch by a slide with slanting top. "Schoolmasters'" desks were also made. Writing tablets were sometimes hinged to the wall.

PLATE 38
Lap- or table-desk

THE desk rests on a "table" made at Canterbury. The top of the stand (29½ inches by 19½ inches) has end cleats and overlaps the frame nearly six inches at each end. Height: 25⅝ inches. Wood: maple and pine. Piece originally painted a dull red.

Though the holy orders forbade "portable writing desks" in the year 1841, Elisha Blakeman, Orren Haskins and other New Lebanon joiners had for a number of years been making lap-desks or "writing-boxes." It is probable that these pieces were first made for sale rather than domestic use, and twenty-five years later the Church deaconesses were replenishing the stock of the office store with desks from the Maine societies. Their frequent appearance in present-day Shaker homes indicates, however, that they were not wholly rejected by the Believers themselves. In fact, an item in the *New Lebanon Ministry Sisters Journal* (Vol. I), under date of Sept. 13, 1834, implies their acceptability in the following regulation:

Rule for making writing boxes, 22 inches long, 15 inches wide and six deep. 1 drawer for paper 1 for an inkstand. If any desire it they may be made slanting.

The frames of Shaker lap-desks are pine, planed to three-eighths of an inch; the members forming the till, the interior partitions and the fronts of the ink-drawers usually measure in thickness only a quarter of an inch; and the sides of these drawers are a fragile eighth of an inch. All joinings are dovetailed, and tiny wooden pulls equip all drawers. The color is a uniform red or yellow. The presence of music sheets and staff-pens in the drawers of many such desks indicates that they may have been used in composing songs.

BEDS AND COTS

PLATES 39–40

THE retiring-room registered the purity of Shaker culture and its conflict with life "on the Adamic plane" more accurately than any other place. The communal meeting-rooms and dining halls, and, to a less extent, the kitchens and various workrooms, possessed certain essential, permanent furnishings; but in the retiring-room, the closer relationship existing between the individual and property presented a temptation to indulge personal tastes. It was probably to combat such a natural instinct for expression and possession that the Millennial Laws regulated the furnishing of the retiring-chambers, but made no reference to uniformity or restraint in other rooms. Individual ownership of property, abrogated in the fundamental covenant, was apparently not always an easy principle to uphold.

Particularly in the Church orders of various societies, where the tenets of Shakerism were most jealously guarded, did the elders constantly labor to keep uncorrupted the ideals of "joint interest."

A record of this struggle is contained in a "roll" written by inspiration in the First Order at New Lebanon on Feb. 5, 1841, which reads in part:

YOUNG brethren and sisters scarce ever consider, that they are not their own, that their *time* is not their own, and that what they get to make their little various notions of is nothing that belongs to them. They do not wait for the gifts of the Ministry and Elders, or Deacons to feel, whether such, and such like things will be necessary, and needful in the family, and thus be provided in order, and all fare alike, as the true order of the Church is established.

Nay; some one is gathered into the Church from an order back, perhaps from the young believers' order, or from some other Society. They bring with them a writing desk, or cupboard, or chest, or case of drawers, made more in fashion or convenient, than has ever been made in the first order.

Some are always ready to take the advantage of a thing like this, and spend days and days, to provide themselves with a piece of furniture, likened to what is brought in, from an order back of them, with a little increase of convenience, on the same plan. Then they are ready to say, "the time was their own, that they took to make the article. I gained it, and I had a right to it."

Then the word is, "*My writing desk! my chest, my tools! my Book! my bench!* etc." And the same spirit exists equally—among the sisters, tho' what they have, is of less importance.

In the Millennial Laws of 1845, it was expressly stated that cupboards, chests, cases of drawers, tables, chairs, trunks, stands, lamps, looking glasses, carpets, mats, beds and bedding shall not be owned "as private property, or individual interest."

The development of Shakerism from a condition of poverty to one of comparative well-being, and thence to one where conformity was subordinated to a degree of worldly comfort and personal convenience, is well illustrated by the bed. At Niskeyuna, in 1788, the Believers had "but little house room, and, of course, had to lie upon the floor, having no convenience for lodging. Fifteen of us laid upon the floor in one room; some had one blanket to cover them,

while others had none, and nought for a pillow but a handkerchief, or a chair turned down so as to recline upon its back."*

PLATE 39
Nurse-shop or infirmary scene

HUNDREDS of cots, painted green and equipped with wooden rollers, were made at New Lebanon as well as at Hancock, where the example illustrated was found. The early cord "bed-steads" were seldom over 6 feet long and 3 feet wide. This one has an outside length of 73¼ inches and an outside width of 33¼ inches. Height to the top of the rails is 17 inches. Height of the headposts (including the roller) is 29½ inches, and of the footposts, 19½ inches. The cotton summer counterpane (white with a brown check) was woven at Sabbathday Lake, Maine.

The electrostatic machine, used for therapeutic purposes by the Shakers at an early date, was found in a shop at the Second family, New Lebanon. According to the *New Lebanon Ministry Sisters Journal*, "the first electrical machine made in the Church was put in operation" on Dec. 17, 1808. The legs and stretchers of the case are delicately turned, and the case finely dovetailed. A domed cover to protect the machine when not in use is not shown in the picture.

The first beds at Hancock and New Lebanon were nothing more than folding cots, sticks of ash, oak or hickory crossed, pinned and held open by cords, or by strips of heavy linen cloth stretched over and securely nailed to the length rails. Soon, however, the opportunity for better accommodation arrived, and the Shakers started making a modified type of cottage or "hired-man's"

*"Reminiscences of Jonathan Clark of Harvard." In *The Shaker*, September, 1871, Vol. I, No. 9, p. 68.

bed—simple affairs with headboards but no footboards, the legs plainly turned and rounded at the top and gradually tapered below the section entered by the cross and length rails. (Plate 39.) Wooden casters, which revolved on a wooden pin inserted into a sturdy fixture doweled into the leg-post, made it possible to roll the cots away from the wall when the sisters made them up in the morning. The posts of later beds were set into cast-iron fixtures collared at the top and slotted at the base to fit over an iron pin in the roller.

In pursuance of the holy laws and ordinances, these "nun-like" beds were invariably painted green: in one community at least, a dark shade for the common members, and a brighter, lighter green for the ministry. The orders continue: "Comfortables should be of a modest color" (in one version "a brownish shade"). "Blankets for outside spreads should be blue and white, but not checked or striped; other kinds now in use may be worn out." Wool was used in the winter, and cotton spreads in the summer; the linen sheets and pillows were "spotless white."

Members were directed to "retire to rest in the fear of God, without any playing, or boisterous laughing, and should lie straight." All were required to rise in the morning at the "signal time," half-past four in the summer and an hour later in winter, "kneel together in silent prayer, stripp from the beds the coverlets and blankets, lighten the feathers, [and] open the windows to ventilate the rooms." "In fifteen minutes . . . the brethren shall leave their rooms" to do early morning chores, and "in half an hour after the bell rings the sisters may go to the brethren's rooms to make the beds etc." Breakfast was served an hour and a half after rising.

PLATE 40
Bed and washstand

THE maple-and-pine bed in Plate 40 belongs to a slightly later period than the one shown in the preceding picture. It is unusually low, but otherwise representative of the cots made at New Lebanon a decade or two before the Civil War. The wood no longer is painted, but treated with a thin stain or varnish, and springs have supplanted rope. The rollers, however, have been retained. The example shown is 6 feet, 2 inches long and 3 feet wide (outside measurements). The headposts are 23 inches in height; the footposts, 17 inches. The counterpane is for summer use, woven in a check of white and two shades of blue. A Shaker-made coat hanger is suspended from a peg.

The pine washstand, stained a light orange color, is one of many simple designs used by the Believers. It is $24\frac{1}{2}$ inches long and 14 inches deep. Height: to flat top, 27 inches; to top of front board, 29 inches; to top of backboard, $27\frac{3}{4}$ inches.

The pine towel rack is from the Church family, New Lebanon. It is 48 inches high and $19\frac{3}{4}$ inches wide; the posts are $1\frac{1}{4}$ inches square. Folding racks with horizontal members mortised through the uprights, and racks with arched feet and branching arms were more common than the one here shown.

The washroom or anteroom connects directly with the retiring-room. Note the trim simplicity of the doorcasing.

Washstands and sinks. Practically nonexistent in the Pilgrim century, and adhering to no standardized forms during the late colonial period, the washstand (often called a "wash-bench") offered an opportunity for multiple, original designs. The high regard for personal and domestic cleanliness, inherent in the tenets of the sect and expressed in numerous matters relating to hygiene, sanitation, ventilation and diet, was symbolized by the presence of one of these pieces in every retiring-room—though it was considered so essential a fixture as not to be included in the Millennial Laws' enumeration of articles for this chamber.

Kitchens, laundries and shops were provided with stone sinks or basins hewn out of native marble and set on hardwood frames. Some were long, but smaller ones were made for entrance halls and sundry work-rooms. A rectangular block was common, but on occasion the tops were chiseled into triangles or half-circles. When immense slabs with smoothly polished surfaces were placed on squared, splayed, maple posts for cellar or dairy use, the retained cold of the stone served as a natural refrigerator. In such pieces, longitudinal braces, mortised and tenoned into the legs, helped to sustain the weight of the stone.

CLOCKS

PLATES 41–42

WATCHES were "contrary to order" among the Shakers until the late 1830's. "To supply every member with a watch," the elders explained, "would be expensive, and if a few were allowed them, others pleading the prerogative of equality, must have them, hence as umbrellas and watches would be useless to many, it was deemed political not to allow them to any."* In another testimony of the period, watches were condemned as "unnecessary indulgences": "if you do not strip them off while in time, when they enter the world of spirits, they will have to be striped off before the holy Angels and justified spirits, to their shame mortification and disgrace." At the Church family, New Lebanon, the need for some kind of portable time-piece was relieved in 1849 by the introduction of "spring or balance clocks," but apparently few were used. As late as 1860 only six watches were in use at this family.

The indispensability of clocks, on the other hand, preserved this article of furniture from prescription. "The clock is an emblem of a Shaker community," an Ohio elder once said, "because everything goes on time . . . Promptness, absolute punctuality, is a *sine qua non* of a successful community."† But even these timekeepers were sparingly used, and at first only in halls. They were made with no attempt at embellishment, and when purchased from the world, had "all their superficial decorations erased from their surfaces."

PLATE 41

Shaker tall-clock, with table and chair
THE clock was found in a Church family shop, but was probably used in a dwelling. The wood is pine, stained or painted red. The hood, which rests on a molding at the top of the case, is 15 inches high, 14 inches long or wide and 8 inches deep. The case, exclusive of hood, is 12 inches wide and 7

*Haskett, William J. *Shakerism Unmasked*, p. 168.

†*The Manifesto*, June, 1887, p. 138.

inches deep. The total height of clock is 6 feet, 9 inches.

Splay-leg drop-leaf tables are rare in Shaker communities. This one is from the New Lebanon Church. Its top, with the leaves down, is 11⅝ inches wide, and with leaves up, 27¾ inches. The table is 36¼ inches long and 26⅛ inches high. Wood: apparently maple, stained a reddish-brown.

PLATE 42
Shaker wall-clock and counter

THE clock is the work of Isaac N. Youngs of New Lebanon: No. 21 in his series. It is 10 inches wide by 3⅝ inches deep by 31 inches high. The wood is walnut. Clock No. 22, shown in Plate 16, is an exact duplicate except for the paneled door.

The counter was used in a weave-room in the sisters' shop at the New Lebanon Church. It is pine, originally painted red, and is unusual because of its top and base molding. Dimensions: 68 inches by 17½ inches by 33 inches. Dark green, blown jars were used in the Shaker extract and medicinal herb industry.

OVAL BOXES. SMALL CABINETWORK AND WOODENWARE
PLATES 43–45

PLATE 43
Oval Boxes

OVAL boxes exemplify, in their shapely compactness and peculiarly satisfying form, that identity of the useful with the beautiful so characteristic of Shaker craftsmanship. To the Believer, a box was more than an enclosure or a receptacle, to be crudely nailed together to answer an immediate need; construction must be painstaking, even in so common an object, if its true usefulness were to be insured. The geometric grace and simplicity of such pieces are symbolical of a people's urge for perfection, even in that work of the hands which was to go forth into the world.

Construction was errorless. A broad, thin band of maple was cut at one end, by means of a template, into "lappers" or "fingers"; the piece was then steamed, wrapped around an oval mold, and the projecting fingers secured by copper or wrought-iron rivets. Discs of pine were then fitted into the base and cover. First made about 1798, oval boxes are still manufactured at New Lebanon and Sabbathday Lake. Formerly they were sold in graduated sizes or "nests," and if equipped with handles were known as "carriers." When colors were used instead of varnish, the reds and yellows, and the rarer blues or greens, were of the mellowest hue. The yellow or orange spit-boxes (Plate 16) were made the same way, sometimes with a rim at the top.

Small cabinetwork and woodenware. The Shaker love of order is evidenced by the great numbers of pine boxes and racks produced in every society of Believers. Wood-boxes, chip-boxes, pipe-boxes and pipe-racks have already been mentioned. Hat-boxes, as we have noted, were fitted inside with four long, turned pegs on which the brethren's felt or colt's-fur hats were hung when not in use. Rectangular dustboxes with central handles flanked by two hinged lids were used in certain families to save frequent emptyings of the dustpans. Candle, cutlery and sewing boxes were dovetailed, lidded, and often molded at the base. Berry-boxes were shaped like an inverted, truncated pryamid, with air holes in each side; vegetable boxes for kitchen use were similarly shaped, but broader and more shallow. Thousands of long shallow boxes were used in the garden-seed business and other kinds in other industries. Tool and storage boxes, sometimes equipped with drawers, were the forerunners of chests and cases of drawers.

Racks were equally useful. As brackets attached to the wall or suspended from the wall-pegs, they held mirrors, clocks or lamps. Wooden candle sconces were fitted with curved side-strips to protect the flame from draught. (Plates 11 and 12.) By means of a series of holes bored one above the other on the upright member, a certain type of sconce found in Kentucky may be hung on the pegs at graduated heights. Floor racks for towels were placed in the washrooms adjoining the retiring-room. (Plate 40.) Racks were also applied to the washstands and wood-boxes, and sometimes fastened to the wall.

Adjustable music racks could be attached to a table or stand. Folding racks were used in airing mattresses and blankets. Broad-shelved milk pan and cheese racks, often set on heavy half-trestle shoes, were an indispensable equipment of storage cellars and dairies. Wet clothes were carried to the lines or dryers by handled devices like miniature hayracks. (Plate 46.) Racks were also used to support bonnet or basket forms (Plate 34), to carry tools, to hold books, to dry the boards on which the pies were "slipped" after being baked, and to

desiccate apples, figs, sweet corn, seeds and herbs. Wooden clothes hangers, often labeled with the user's initials, served the cause of order.

Reference has already been made to Shaker wall cupboards. Some were shaped like a mirror or lamp rack, with a compartment instead of a shelf below. In others, the back was extended into a graceful crest. (Plate 13.) Hanging racks of two or three drawers served useful purposes in the kitchens and pantries. The wood was invariably pine.

Woodenware* made for home use rather than for sale included mixing bowls, spoons, rolling pins, trenchers, mortars and pestles, vegetable "shutes," measuring-sticks, knife handles, spools and spool stands, canes, pitcher and medicine-glass covers, table boards for hot dishes, scrubboards, foot warmers, lanterns, clothespins and coffins.

Brush, broom and mop handles were turned in the Shaker shops. On small, beautifully constructed looms, silk or hair was woven for the Shaker sieves, then tightened between the two parts of the rim on special devices called sieve-binders. Braid-looms were used for weaving the straw binding of bonnets, and for chair and carpet braids. The palm leaf, poplar or black ash used in the bonnet and basket industries was woven on larger looms, while the largest of all were needed in weaving cloth and carpeting. Woolwheels, reels, swifts, quill-wheels, bobbin winders, spinning jennies, cards, hatchels, skarns—all were the product of Shaker craftsmanship. (Plate 24.) At Enfield, Connecticut, the pedestal and feet

---

*An abundant supply of wood encouraged the manufacture and use of woodenware. Many devices and utensils ordinarily made of metal were constructed of wood in the community itself.

of clock-reels were like those of a snake-foot candlestand, an aspect of design indicative of the close relationship between the shop and the home.

PLATE 44
Pegs and pulls

EXAMPLES of turned pegs used as drawer pulls. An early wall-peg and a more typical one with threaded flange are shown in the center. Pegs used in the pegboards or peg-rails project from two to three inches from the board.

Small pegs, such as were used on clock doors, the drawers of lap-desks, the sides of washstands, beneath windows, etc., may measure little over half an inch in total length, and a quarter-inch in head diameter. Maple and cherry were the common woods.

PLATE 45
Chair buttons

TURNED maple "buttons" used on Shaker "tilting-chairs." The one at the left, rear, its lower rim almost obliterated by use, is the oldest. The one in the left foreground is made of pewter. These buttons or "balls" were fitted in a socket at the base of the rear chair posts (as illustrated) and joined by a leather or gut thong knotted at the base of the button. The thong passed through a hole bored in the ball and another bored in the post a little over an inch from the bottom. The button rested flat on the floor as the chair took "its natural motion of rocking backward and forward." This device added to the comfort already provided by the slanting back of most Shaker side chairs.

SHOP FURNITURE
PLATES 46–48

THE furnishings of the many workshops used by the early Believers comprise an integral part of the present study. They were often made by the same craftsmen who constructed household furniture, and with no less scrupulous skill. Removed from its setting, shop furniture would often be indistinguishable from that made for the dwelling. The Shaker communal dwelling was in a sense an expansive colonial household, sheltering many industries which, as soon as circumstances permitted, became separately housed. The shop was thus an extension of the home, its activity governed also by a spirit of consecration and the practical Millennial Laws.

The statute books prescribed order and regulated workmanship in these terms:

Brethren shall work in their shops, or other places prepared for them, Sisters in their shops or retiring-rooms.

Sisters shall clean brethren's shops twice a year, and brethren sweep them every day when used and clean the spit boxes.

All the gates should be closed on Saturday night, and work rooms should be swept; the work and tools should be in order, and safely secured from thieves and fire.

Ye shall not leave the rooms where you live nor the shops where you work, without letting some one know where you are going.

No one should take tools, belonging in charge of others, without obtaining liberty for the same, if the person can consistently be found who takes charge of them.

When any one borrows a tool, it should be immediately returned, without injury, if possible, and if injured, should be made known by the borrower to the lender;—"The wicked borrow and never return."

Ye shall not lock the places wherein ye keep tools at the shops, except by the counsel of the Elders.

Joiner's and carpenter's tools and work bench [shall not be owned as private property].

It is the duty of the Elders and Deacons (or leaders) to know that every one is provided with suitable tools to work with, and proper accommodation for carrying on their business.

Give them liberty to make, or get made, any thing that is profitable or necessary.

But no individual shall make, or get made, bring in or cause to be brought in, any new fashioned tool, article, or accomodation, without the full approbation of the leaders of the family.

No one may smoke in their . . . shops under an hour previous to leaving them for the night . . . and no one may smoke and work at the same time.

Believers should not work as hirelings, gaining time to do as they please, but every one should work diligently with their hands, according to their strength, for the public good of the society.

All should be careful not to mar or destroy the furniture in their shops or rooms.

Believers may not in any case, manufacture for sale, any article or articles, which are superfluously wrought, and which would have a tendency to feed the pride and vanity of man, or such as would not be admissible to use among themselves, on account of their superfluity.

Occasion has arisen for mentioning the furniture and fittings of the sisters' weave-shops, nurse-shops, laundries, sewing rooms, tailoring-rooms, herb-shops, dairies and kitchens. The occupations followed by the brethren required less actual furniture, and more mechanical or technical equipment. Mortising machines, herb presses, presses for printing labels, portable electrostatic machines, brush-vises, broom-vises and machines, herb cutters, table-mat presses and cutters, cheese-presses, shingle and stave benches, saddler's chairs, apple-paring benches, butter-workers, mangles and wringers and "wash-mills," leather-cutters and many other machines and laborsaving devices, illustrate the capable workmanship of the mechanic and joiner. The skill expended on the wooden patterns for stoves, arch-covers and doors, wheels and other objects is comparable to that employed on the finest furniture.

PLATE 46
Ironing-room in washhouse of the Hancock church

WITH typical furnishings. Flatirons rest on ridges along the sloping sides of the stove. Water is boiled and clothes are steamed in the brick-enclosed "arch." The laundry counter is also part of the permanent equipment of the room.

To left and right are "starch-tables." The longer one is 41 inches by 29 inches by $27\frac{1}{4}$ inches. The one at the right (holding a keeler) is $27\frac{1}{2}$ inches by $22\frac{1}{2}$ inches by $26\frac{1}{2}$ inches. Both are New Lebanon pieces.

The chair by the window has a single broad slat and square posts which angle slightly backwards just above the seat. The seat is 25 inches above the floor. Similar chairs, some without backs, have been found at New Lebanon and other communities. A clothes-carrier hangs on the pegboard along the further wall.

Many interesting pieces of furniture were used in the old Shaker "washhouses" or laundries. Tubs, benches, drying racks, clothes-carriers, pails, dyeing-troughs, scrubboards, pressing-boards and many other accessories served the cause of cleanliness and efficiency. A wash-mill was invented at New Lebanon and patented in 1858 at Canterbury, where an improved mangle was also devised. A rectangular, bin-shaped table with heavy, turned and raked legs was used at New Lebanon for washing and soapmaking—a primitive forerunner of the set tub. A special kind of laundry table, on which buckets of starch were placed, was made by several families in this community.

PLATE 47
Cobbler's shop

THE scene is the original shoemaker's shop at the Second family of the Church Order, New Lebanon. The cobbler's bench and floor stand for candles were found in a brethren's shop at the Second family. The smaller candlestand was made at the Church. Early lasts were Shaker-made.

A double-paneled lid protects the cabinet of the bench and lets down to serve as a work-tray. A circular scoop on this lid was filled with wax. In the cabinet are variously shaped compartments for tools and a number of small drawers, with delicate bone knobs and tin bottoms for pegs, brads and the trivia of the trade. Two larger drawers, underslung beneath the seat, contained the kit: wooden heels, a blown

blacking-bottle, a foot-measure, "slicking sticks," awls and hafts, punches, pincers, "crooked knife" and leather. The leather-covered baseboard was bound at the sides with brass studs and typically scooped at one end to form a seat, which was usually provided with a back rest. The top of the cabinet frame was dovetailed, as were all the drawers. The cross rails of the doors were mortised and doweled into the side rails, and other parts of the frame were secured by hand-forged screws. The seat and working surface of the bench is $11\frac{1}{2}$ inches above the floor; the height to the top of the cabinet is $33\frac{1}{4}$ inches. The cabinet itself is $25\frac{1}{4}$ inches wide and 10 inches deep, and the total length of the bench, 51 inches. Wood, butternut.

A second requirement for every cobbler's shop was a candlestand. "In-door mechanics," wrote Brown in 1812, "in the winter work by candlelight"—probably on many an evening or early morning. In the machine, carpentry and shoemaking shops, such stands are mute reminders of consecrated toil. The floor stand depicted consists of a threaded, maple stem collared at the base to set into a crude, oak block. A double candle-arm in the shape of a figure "8" allowed the candles to be "burned at both ends," and at a given height. The rounded projections of the arms were banded with a metal rim. The base and post of the small candlestand on top of the bench were turned from a single section of maple, and the arms were rimmed with wood. The tin, iron or steel candlesticks used on these stands were made in Shaker shops.

The cobbler was his own last maker, hewing out from solid blocks patterns to fit the foot of every member in the family. These were kept in racks formed by dovetailing a series of parallel rails into two uprights attached to the wall. At Niske-yuna, the racks were provided with half-trestle shoes.

Shoe leather came from the Shaker tanyard, the cloth (used for sisters' shoes), from the weave-shop. In the earliest regulations of the sect it was "contrary to order to have right and left shoes" or "to pare the heels of the shoes under." Such orders were given "to mortify the pride of the young believers, who, if allowed in these things, would border more and more on the fashions of the world, and by this means return to its beggarly elements."

PLATE 48

Carpenter's bench

IN the brethren's shop at the North family, New Lebanon. Used by the last elder and minister at the central Shaker society. The top of the bench is 112 inches long, $34\frac{1}{4}$ inches wide or deep, and $31\frac{7}{8}$ inches high. The maple top is $3\frac{5}{8}$ inches thick. The lower frame or base (72 inches by 31 inches by $28\frac{1}{4}$ inches) is pine.

Hanging on the pegboard are a high swivel shop stool and a wooden lantern. The seat of the stool is 28 inches high.

The long bench is 50 inches by $13\frac{1}{2}$ inches by 23 inches. Similar ones were made measuring over six feet in length and nearly two feet in width.

All workbenches were liberally supplied with drawers and conveniences. Except for their massive, overhanging tops and vise or screw attachments, many resemble the long counters of other shops. Under the overlapping front of a Watervliet example was a sliding panel, common in old carpenters' or wheelwrights' benches, "with peg holes and a peg for holding up the free end of a board clamped in the vise." Maple was common. Thomas Fisher of Enfield, Connecticut, equipped one drawer of his benches as a desk. A great many were constructed at New Lebanon in the late 1820's, when the two largest brethren's shops were built.

High shop stools are affiliated with the swivel chairs. The legs of the example in Plate 48 are of the "flattened turning," rectangular or chamfered-edge type, the rungs and slats being mortised completely through the posts. The related loom stools had sloping seats, commonly covered with leather, and usually a back rest and a drawer or shelf for holding weaving tools.

APPENDICES

A

The Shaker chair industry

THE Shakers were "pioneers" in the chair industry, and "perhaps the very first to engage in the business after the establishment of the independence of the country."* From 1789, when the first sales were entered in the accounts of the Church trustees at New Lebanon, an intermittent trade was carried on by one family or another at this colony until about 1852, when foundations were laid for the more standardized production which has continued uninterruptedly to the present day.

At New Lebanon, the center of the industry, chair-making passed through three more or less distinct stages: an initial period in which evidences of adaptation are apparent in experimental crudities; a middle period, from early in the last century until the Civil War, when a perfected and traditional style was maintained; and the era of "mass production," from the late fifties on, when design increasingly betrayed the effects of power machines. Numbers of side chairs made in the first period are hardly distinguishable from the rustic, dull-painted slat-backs of the surrounding countryside. Soon, however, craftsmanship began to assume the simple generic character of an accepted style, though the patterns of chairs were not so rigid as to take from the products of the small shops their individuality and quiet purity of form. In the last quar-

ter of the century, however, it was apparent that stereotyped methods had begun to affect the true folk quality of the workmanship.

The three-slat side chair, with its traditional qualities of lightness, grace and unpretentiousness, probably had its origin in that branch of the New Lebanon society which was variously known as the East family, the Hill family, Spiers' or The Brickyard. A brook descending the steep Taconic mountainside was here dammed, supplying power for a mill which produced, until about 1840, most of the chairs used or resold by the large Church family, of which the East order was a branch. The earliest item on record was included in a "bill of articles delivered" by the Church deacons to one Mary Dayley, who left the society Dec. 8, 1788: "6 chairs . . . 1:10:00." On Oct. 21, 1789, according to the trustees' account book at the Church, three chairs were sold to Elijah Slosson, probably the deacon of some other family, for eleven shillings. The following entries cover the next decade:

1790 To Daniel Goodrich (Hancock
   trustee) 4 chairs at 4/8   £0:18:8
May 6 To bottoming 6 chairs (for
   Elizah Sacket)   0: 7:0
1791 Feby Delivered to Eliphelet
   Comstock, in Enfield, Conn . . . 6
   chairs. (no price recorded)
Feby 2 To Eleazer Grant (a magistrate in the town of New Lebanon)
   . . . 6 chairs   1: 0:0
Novr 10 To Zebulon Goodrich 3
   chairs without Bottoms but Painted   0:10:0
1792 Novr 19 To Timothy Edwards

Illustrated catalogue of Shaker chairs, foot benches, floor mats, etc. (By Elder Robert Wagan, South family, Mt. Lebanon, Columbia County, N.Y.) Albany, 1874.

of Stockbridge, Mass. 8 chairs
@ 3/   1: 4:0
1798 One "house Chair" delivered to
John Shapley   0: 5:0

Sometime in the last decade of the eighteenth century the Believers began distributing their manufactures to country stores in the vicinity and to larger concerns in Albany, Troy, Hudson, Granville (New York) and Poughkeepsie. In one-horse wagons the Shaker peddlers, Nathan and Stephen Slosson, made trips even as far as Boston or New York, carrying such merchandise as garden seeds, leather, sheep and calf skins, brooms, brushes, dippers, pails, whips and whiplashes, wire and hair sieves, nests of oval boxes, machine cards, spinning-wheels, hoes, vegetables and chairs. From these trading centers the driver would return with his collections on "dubils" and necessities not produced by the Shakers themselves. A few chair items are selected from the records of these early deliveries:

1805 Sept. 18 Sold 4 Chairs @ 6/   £1: 4:0
          23 Sold 1 Wagain Chair*   0:14:0
             Do 1 Rocking Chair   0:16:0
             Nathan Rec'd for Al-
bany . . . 3 chairs   0:19:0
          2 Wagain Do @ 14/6   1: 9:0
          27 Sold to John Tryon
(an early storekeeper in the village
of New Lebanon) 12 Chairs @ 6 at
10 pr. Cent reduction. (For which
the Church received in exchange "1

Gall. Sherry wine; 1 Do Malaga Do; 6 lb. Rasons; 3 Chambers; 8 Milkpans" and thirteen shillings, eleven pence.)
1806 Feb. 12 Stephen Rec'd for hudson . . . 34 chairs at 6/   10: 4:0
Mar. 25 Nathan Rec'd for Lansbory (Lanesborough, Mass.) . . . 9 chairs @ 6/4   2:17:0
Mar. 21 Sold 2 wagain Chairs 14 & 12   1: 6:0
Aug. 9 Nathan Rec'd for Hudson . . . 12 Wagain Chairs @ 14   8: 8:0
Aug. 30 Sold Rocking Chair 16/ & 1 Wagain Chair 13/   1: 9:0
Sept. 25 Stephen Rec'd for hudson 10 Small chairs 4/6   2: 5:0
1807 Feb. 26 Paid Asa Talcot for 12 Chairs which was set off Against the Timber they [i.e. the East family] had Recd to make Chairs
Marc. 2 Sold 2 Small Chairs @ 5/   0:10:0
     16 Sold to John Tryon 6 Chairs .75 $4.50
April 7 Rec'd of Dc. Samuel [Samuel Ellis, an East family deacon] 2 high Chairs without Botoms @ 4/ $1.00
1809 June 13 Nathan Rec'd for Granvail [Granville, N. Y.] 1 Small Chair   .56

The absence of entries in the accounts of the succeeding years indicates that manufacture for some reason lapsed, or perhaps that the total output was utilized by the rapidly growing community. In 1814, the chair-makers' shop, probably the "factory" at the East family, was destroyed by a heavy storm and flood which swept away "a large number of unfinished chairs, stock and tools."[†] This "catastrophe" may have been responsible for the few sales recorded during the next fifteen years. From 1829 to 1839, the Church trustees were again purchasing a considerable quantity of frames from Thomas Estes, the East family

---

*The wagon chair ("wagain" in the records) was apparently an adaptation of the colonial oxcart or wagon seat. It was a low double "chair," with two slats on each side. (See Andrews, Edward D.: The Community Industries of the Shakers, Plate 62, p. 235.) Since the frame fitted snugly within the wagon box, legs were not required. The boarded seat and often the slats were padded with hair covered with leather. The one-horse wagon, a contribution to American transportation credited to the Shakers, was equipped with these seats, and many were sold by the New Lebanon Church, early in the last century, at a price varying from twelve to fifteen shillings each.

†New Lebanon Ministry Sisters Journal, Vol. I, 1780–1891. Entry for August 28, 1814.

deacon, and from his successor, William Thrasher. With the advent of the revised currency in 1807, the price per side chair was changed to seventy-five cents, a charge maintained for over thirty years.

Chairs in sets of three, six or twelve were carefully matched, but designs, even within a given community, varied in size, height, color and finial turning. The production of special types like "small chairs" and "great chairs" indicates also that the process was not inflexible. Strength and durability were insured by the use in the posts of carefully selected and seasoned hard maple, sometimes curly or bird's-eye. Cherry, birch and butternut were used less often. The slats of the earliest chairs were invariably maple; the rungs were ash, hickory, or maple. The acorn-shaped knobs were sometimes pointed, but more often rounded on top, occasionally assuming a ball-like pattern. Narrow splint was universally employed in the first chair seats; at times leather was used, and cane, tape, rush or "plaited straw" were not uncommon at a later period. Most of the earliest side chairs and rockers were painted dark red, but soon the custom prevailed of staining the wood with a thin red or yellow wash. Varnish stains, copal varnish, aqua vitae and chrome yellow mixed with shellac were later favored, and finally dark-colored commercial dyes into which the frames were dipped.

ROCKING CHAIRS

THE Believers were probably the first people in this country to produce and use the rocking chair on a systematic scale. Intended originally for aged or infirm sisters or brethren, it was not long before such chairs were assigned to every retiring-room in the family dwelling, evidence that Shaker asceticism did not exclude a modicum of comfort and convenience. Few rocking chairs were made at New Lebanon, however, before 1800, and only three are included in a total of nearly three hundred chairs manufactured in the period 1805–07. The original price of sixteen shillings had advanced by 1830 to $2.50; and "easy chairs," if seated in splint, still sold for this amount in 1860. The frames alone were priced at a shilling less, and fifty cents more if equipped with tape or webbed seats. "Common" rocking chairs, that is, chairs without arms, were vended in 1831 for a dollar apiece.

Like the early side chairs, rockers were made to no fixed pattern, though they may be arbitrarily classified into five groups: the mushroom post type, the scrolled-arm type, the type with rolled arms, the cushion-rail chair and the sewing rocker. To the first three classes belong most of the early Shaker armchairs. All have four slats, one rung at the rear and two at the front and sides; the arm rests usually are low, giving an impression of height to the chairs which was accentuated by the comparatively narrow backs and the long finials. (*See* Plate 30.) The scrolled and rolled arms and the mushroom post were appropriations from colonial craftsmanship. In the earliest chairs (note Plate 16) the scroll (sometimes called by the Shakers a "ladle-arm") was crudely fashioned, though soon the form was a graceful curve. The front posts tapered slightly above the seat rail and were turned an inch or so beneath the arm end to form a small collar. (Plate 16.) The rolled arm, particularly characteristic of Harvard and Shirley craftsmanship (though found at Canterbury and elsewhere), was molded and curved, and terminated in an abbreviated or complete roll. In a variant type produced at Hancock the arm was rolled and doweled into the front post to form an unbroken curve.

The mushroom post, used almost exclusively in the later Shaker chairs, was common at an early period. At first the wide, gently crested, flat-bottomed mushrooms were turned in the same piece with the rest of the front post, whose diameter slightly decreased above the rail of the seat and assumed its original dimensions in a collar just below the arm. (Plates 14 and 27.) The arms were flat, strong, moderately curved and cut at the end to fit part way around the post, just beneath the mushroom. In the later rockers a more slender post was turned above the seat into the lovely sweep of an urn, the top of which penetrated a hole bored in the arm, the mushroom being applied as a separate piece. (Plates 7 and 15.) As the century advanced, however, the turning of the posts was unvaried, the mushroom assumed a disproportionate smallness and heavy, onion-shaped form, and the arms an angular, uninteresting pattern. The finial also disintegrated into a weak knob obtained by merely grooving the back posts near the top and tapering off the end.

The passage of time is similarly recorded in the rockers. The earliest type fitted into sockets or slots cut in the posts, which were sometimes heavily collared at the base to give added strength. The rockers did not extend beyond the front post, and terminated five to seven inches at the back. High cradle-shaped or "sled" rockers were also used, especially on brethren's chairs, in which cases the posts were slotted the full width of the rocker. Sometimes in armchairs, and generally in the sewing rockers, the posts were tapered at the bottom and doweled into the top of narrow, short rockers made of maple, hickory or ash. The tendency was first to shape the rocker more carefully, then to lengthen it, and finally to cut it in a long "knife-blade" pattern often no more than three-eighths of an inch in thickness.

The age of rocking chairs may also be roughly determined by the shape and placement of dowels. Irregular, square-shaped dowels, chiseled out by hand, secured the slats of all types of early chairs. In rockers, both the top slat and the one above the bottom were pegged into the post, usually from the rear; and in the earliest New Lebanon types dowels were used on the two upper slats. Sometimes the upper chair slats were doweled both front and rear. The later custom was to peg only the top slat or to depend entirely on glue.

To increase the comfort of the growing number of aged or infirm members, certain innovations in the style and seats of rocking chairs were made about 1830. Colored tapes or braid (sometimes called list or listing when the selvage of textiles was used), woven in a checkerboard pattern, partially displaced the splint seats and were later used to "upholster" the back also. That side chairs were also equipped with listed seats is indicated by the number of pieces billed from the East family, between 1830 and 1840, as "fraims" only. Henry DeWitt, a Church family joiner, constructed his tape looms during this period; and in 1841, when the "Orders Rules and Counsels for the People of God" were compiled, reference was made to "Plain split, beark [bark], list or tape bottomed chairs." Braids with over fifty color combinations were woven on these special-type looms, or on cloth looms equipped with an attachment so that as many as seven tapes could be simultaneously produced. About 1832, the sisters at the Church family also started to make chair cushions or "mats," which were used on the splint-seat chairs and sold to other societies. The increasing emphasis on ease* resulted, toward mid-century, in the cushion-rail chair, structurally similar to the four-slat armchair, but provided with a curved rod which joined the tops of the back posts and displaced the "pommels." (Plates 7 and 8.) A soft mat of plush or "shag" was suspended from this rail and a similar one attached to the seat.

The trend toward lightness and comfort is further exhibited by the narrower turning of posts whose diameter in many mid-century rockers barely exceeds an inch, and an occasional backward bend of the rear posts achieved by steaming these members and drying them in a form. The slats and arms were also more thinly planed, the former in some cases to less than a quarter-inch, the latter to slightly more than half an inch. Wider seats became more common. The mushroom decreased in diameter and was sometimes turned with a flat rim and mounded center. The finials, representing in the early chairs free interpretations of the acorn, conformed to a more outright but not unpleasing pattern; and the tilting-balls were more delicately turned. The low-seated sewing chairs, which were contemporary with the armed

rocker, were raised in height and provided with arms and the applied mushroom. Though a certain primitive sturdiness was lost in these "improvements," such was the harmony of parts, the graceful simplicity of the completed piece, and the colorful brightness achieved by the natural finish and varicolored seat tapes, that chairs made just prior to the period of standardized deterioration may be classed among the most charming examples of Shaker craftsmanship.

LATE PERIOD CHAIRS

In the middle of the last century the chair business at New Lebanon was concentrated in the Second and Canaan families at the south end of this large community. James Farnum, John Lockwood and Gilbert Avery, the best-known chair-makers of the time, were laying the foundations of a prosperous industry in a little shop on the Canaan road and in a power mill on Cherry Lane, in the Shaker village itself. Its supervisors were the Second family elders, Daniel Hawkins and D. Clinton Brainard, and the energetic Robert Wagan, later to become leading elder at the South family. Associated with these brethren was George O. Donnell, who, in 1852, took out a government patent† on the tilting-chair device—evidence of a serious interest in manufacture as a busi-

---

*During the great revival of 1837–1847, the conflict between the strong Shaker sense of convenience and the impulse to abide by rigid principles of sanctity, found expression in several "testimonies" against rocking chairs. An interesting example of such inspired communication is that delivered on April 11, 1840 by the instrument Philemon Stewart, speaking in the name of the Holy Father and Holy Mother Wisdom. "How comes it about [says this message in part] that there are so many rocking chairs used? Is the rising generation going to be able to keep the way of God, by seeking after ease?" (From a message delivered to the ministry and elders at the First Order of the Church, New Lebanon, April 11, 1840. MS.)

†Patent No. 8771, "Improvement in Chairs." In filing his claim for a patent, Donnell stated that his invention (obviously based on the early wooden ball-and-socket) was "the construction and application of a metallic combination to the back posts of chairs, so as to let the chairs take their natural motion of rocking backwards and forwards, while the metallic feet rest unmoved flat and square on the floor or carpet." (See *Report of the Commissioner of Patents for the year* 1852. Part I. Arts and Manufactures.) Apparently the brass or composition "ferrule, ball, and foot piece" was used on very few Shaker chairs. (See Plate 37.) The Shakers seldom patented their inventions, as they believed that patent money savoured of monopoly.

ness. By the end of the fifties, orders amounting to as high as $150 point to a definitely accelerated production.

The chairs made in this middle period were closely related to early-century types. But deterioration in workmanship began with the inception, during the Civil War, of a well-organized industry marked by standardized processes and laborsaving machinery, and catering directly to popular taste. In March, 1863, "the South house," formerly a branch of the Second family, became an independent order, with Robert Wagan as its elder. A stock of 432 chairs, which included armed rockers, "broad seat" easy rockers, "high back" easy chairs, armchairs without rockers, dining chairs with arms, piano stools and children's "revolvers" (amounting to $889) was left to be disposed of at the Second family's office and store.

Two weeks later Wagan started seriously to reorganize the business. He purchased a wood lathe, iron lathe, boring machine, planer and "dressing machine"; planned production so that chairs could be made and sold according to size and number; and began operations immediately. Business followed in the wake of advertising. A large order came from the Church family in 1866. Wholesale orders from concerns in New York, Philadelphia, Boston and other cities entered the books in 1867. Two years later annual production had reached 600 chairs ($2,400), and Elder Robert had replaced the old shop with a water-power "factory." But even this establishment apparently could not meet the increased demand, for in 1872 he erected another factory, purchasing "a thousand dollar engine . . . to drive the machinery." Two years later the first chair catalogues were issued. Elder Robert died in 1883,

but the occupation of chair-making at the South, and later at the Second family, continued to flourish, and only within the last few years has dwindled as a result of unavoidable misfortunes in an almost extinct order.

Three types of chairs were advertised in the catalogues of the last quarter of the century: upholstered, web-back and slatback. These could be had with or without arms, cushion rails or rockers. Chair frames and "foot benches" were also sold, and at a later date small chairs with rod backs. Cushions came in fourteen colors, and in 1876 were still being "woven in hand looms with much labor." Many of the web-back chairs, with their varicolored checkerboard effects, were appealing creations: an ebony chair, for instance, done in red and black tapes, or a chair finished "white" in the natural color of the maple, with green and taupe listing. The lightness of these late examples of Shaker craftsmanship is witnessed by the cataloger's assertion: "Our largest chairs do not weigh over ten pounds, and the smallest weigh less than five pounds, and yet the largest person can feel safe in sitting down in them without fear of going through them."*

Wagan chairs, and those made after his death (under the supervision of Elder William Anderson), deserve attention as symbols of conflict between worldliness and established traditions of craftsmanship. Some of the new forms which Elder Robert created have indubitable merit: in fact, the designs themselves did not clash with Shaker conventions as much as did the subtle qualities of the workmanship. The mushrooms on armchairs, for instance, conformed to a set pattern; lathe marks were

*Centennial Illustrated Catalogue and Price List of the Shakers' Chairs, etc. Albany, 1876, p. 9.

not smoothed out; and the posts, caliper-turned and often steamed to an unsatisfactory curve, lack the evidence of individualized labor. The trade-mark ("in ornamental gold transfer") was adopted because inferior imitations were being widely marketed.

The "upholstering" of chairs in bright-colored tapes and plushes also indicates a partial capitulation to worldly ways of fostering enterprise. Whereas in the early tape seats soft colors were prescribed and variety of color limited, "R. M. Wagan and Co." offered fourteen colors: black, navy blue, peacock blue, light blue, maroon, pomegranate, brown, grass green, dark olive, light olive, old gold, drab, scarlet and orange. Instead of finishing the frames as the early Shakers did, the chair-makers aimed at imitation mahogany or "old walnut" colors, dipping the assembled pieces in vats of hot logwood dye to get the former color, and treating the wood with aqua fortis to get the latter.*

The chairs produced at New Lebanon since the Civil War retained, nevertheless, much of the charm and restraint of early Shaker joinery. It is often difficult to distinguish an 1870 chair from one made twenty or thirty years earlier; and the essential style of side chairs and many rocker types (combining, to use the catalogue phrase, "the advantages of durability, simplicity and lightness") persisted long after the Wagan period. In 1876, when examples of the Shaker chairs were exhibited at the Philadelphia Centennial, they were considered refreshing novelties of the Victorian period, and won a diploma and medal for their "Strength, Sprightliness and Modest Beauty." The catalogues issued for this occasion were "sent out as a tract, greeting the people, wishing them well, calling them to repentance, and then giving the pictures of the chairs which the community at Mount Lebanon had made."† The inclusion of several Shaker songs in this pamphlet illustrates how intimately the religion of the Believers was identified with their workmanship.

Chair-making for profit was followed in other Shaker societies, notably the Harvard and Canterbury communities. Apparently every eastern society made its own chairs, though identifiable deviations in early design rarely distinguish the product of a given society. The long, simple finials of the Enfield, New Hampshire, types were duplicated at Canterbury, at the Maine settlements, and at Harvard and Shirley. A peculiarly delicate finial turning was employed at a certain period by the Hancock chair-makers, and a somewhat distinctive form at Alfred and Sabbathday Lake. The rungs in a certain type constructed at the latter community have the slightly swollen turning of the bamboo Windsors. But such clues to origin are meagre and unreliable. All side chairs had three slats, all rockers four; and tilting-chairs were made in many communities.

B

Notes on Benjamin and Isaac Youngs, Shaker clockmakers

A CLOCKMAKER was at work at the New Lebanon community as early as 1790, when

---

*After the logwood dye process, the frames were hung on wall-pegs to dry. The walnut or "cherry" colors were set by constant turning of the frames before a hot fire. According to a South family record, the less frequent ebony finish was obtained by boiling logwood and cider together "in iron," adding water "for the evaporation," and "setting" the black with copperas. Sometimes ink powder was used, sometimes "rusty nails, or any bits of rusty iron, boiled in vinegar."

†Ferguson, C. W. *The Confusion of Tongues*. Chapter on Shakerism.

a record occurs (March 22) of a clock and case sold for 8/4 to one Nathan Farrington, a farmer living in the northwestern part of the town. On April 10 a "timepiece" was repaired, and on May 19, Amos Hammond, a later leader in the Church, purchased another for 1/12. Three clocks were said to have been in use at this family in 1792, the number increasing to seven in 1796. "To each dwelling," Haskett later reported, "is attached an alarum clock."

The clocks mentioned were undoubtedly made by Amos Jewett, one of the first Believers at New Lebanon, which in the 1790's was part of the township of Canaan, New York. An extant example of Jewett's work, a tall case clock in pine, is inscribed on the dial: "1796/Amos Jewett/Canaan/No. 38" —a serial number indicating that the craftsman's output was not limited. The records of the New Lebanon Church list Jewett's death on March 18, 1834, at the age of 81.*

Most of the earliest Shaker clocks, however, were produced at the Niskeyuna or Watervliet community, which was fortunate to include in its membership a skilled Connecticut clockmaker by the name of Benjamin Youngs. This craftsman was born in Hartford on September 23, 1736, the eldest son of Seth Youngs, a maker of timepieces who may have learned his trade from Ebenezer Parmele, the "father" of clockmaking in Connecticut. Apparently Benja-

min was apprenticed to his father in Windsor, where the latter had moved in 1742. At the time of his death in 1761, Seth Youngs left all his working tools to his three eldest sons, Joseph, Benjamin and Seth. Benjamin worked at silversmithing and clockmaking in Windsor until 1766, when he moved to Schenectady, New York. "In 1767 he was in Capt. Nicholas Groots' Company of Militia," writes the genealogist of the Youngs family, adding that "in 1806, he removed with his family to Watervliet, N.Y., where they all joined the Shaker community."

A letter from Freegift Wells, written from Wisdom's Valley (Niskeyuna) on March 8, 1871, quotes the Church records to the effect that "Benjamin Youngs confessed his sins in 1792, while still living with his family in Schenectady.... In 1794, he moved his family to Watervliet on a farm adjoining, and located South and East of the farm possessed by the Church, and on which their little village stood.... It appears that Benjamin purchased this farm some time previous to moving. Thus it appears that Benjamin Youngs Sen. and wife, were the first who set out to be Believers, in what is termed the second opening of the Gospel." Benjamin's nephew, Benjamin S. Youngs, the son of his brother Seth and brother to Isaac N. Youngs (of whom more hereafter), was one of the three Shaker missionaries sent out by the New Lebanon ministry in 1805 "to open the gospel" in Ohio and Kentucky. There he wrote "The Testimony of Christ's Second Appearing," in which the principles of the Church were first "laid open from their proper source and foundation." Benjamin, Sr., the clockmaker, died on Oct. 30, 1818.

Comparison of Benjamin Youngs's wall- and floor clocks with those made by his

*Little information is available about this craftsman's life. That he was an early disciple of Mother Ann is proved by the fact that he was one of the "living witnesses" whose *Testimonies of the life, character, revelations and doctrines of our ever blessed mother Ann Lee, and the elders with her* were published in 1816. In this work he testifies as follows (p. 330): "Mother asked young Joseph Bennet, which he thought had the greatest gift, of the two Elders, William or James. 'I think [answered Joseph] that Elder William has the greatest gift of sorrow.' 'So he has'; replied Mother; 'James plants and William waters.'"

father and other craftsmen in the Connecticut tradition, graphically illustrates the effect of the Shaker religion on craftsmanship. In his later work, all excess ornament is lacking, and only in the arched pediment and door, the slender columns and mechanism of the floor clocks and the finely wrought hands and dial figures of the wall- or shelf clocks, are the training and taste of his early years faintly reflected. "Grandmother's" clocks were an important item in Youngs's output, as were the "alarum clocks" sent out to many Shaker societies about 1812. One of the former, in the possession of the Western Reserve Historical Society, measures a little over three feet in height and is about eight inches wide—the hood an inch or so wider. The dial is numbered in both Roman and arabic numerals, and inscribed "Benjamin Youngs, Watervliet." In a Youngs floor clock made in 1806 and still in use at the New Lebanon village,* the name of the society is spelled "Water Vliet." Both cases are of cherry. The red-painted pine clock in Plate 41, possibly from the same hand, has an even simpler case, the vertical lines being broken only by a quarter-round molding at the base and top and the plain, concave molding which supports the hood.

Family tradition affected the early interests of Benjamin's nephew, Isaac N. Youngs, the chief clockmaker at New Lebanon. Born at Johnston, New York, July 2 [4?], 1793, the son of Seth Youngs and Martha Farley, he was brought to the Niskeyuna community when but six months old. At the age of seven or eight, according to "his history in verse"† written in 1837,

*Illustrated in the magazine *Antiques*, April, 1929, p. 296, Plate 12.
†Isaac Newton Youngs. "His History in Verse," July 4, 1837. MS.

To read in books I much desir'd,
To skill in clocks I too aspir'd
In making dams and woodmills too . . .

And, as a boy,

'Twas here that I did undertake
A little wooden clock to make,
But Abigail Richardson
Burnt it all up.

At the age of fourteen, Isaac moved to the New Lebanon society and was immediately engaged in the versatile and crowded occupational life of all early Shaker mechanics. As he quaintly wrote:

I'm overrun with work and chores
Upon the farm or within doors
Which ever way I turn my eyes;
Enough to fill me with surprise.
How can I bear with such a plan?
No time to be a gentleman!
All work—work—work, still rushing on,
And *conscience* too still pushing on:
When will the working all be done?
When will this lengthy thread be spun?
As long as *working* is the cry
How can I e'er find time to die?

.   .   ..

Of tayl'ring, Join'ring, farming too,
Almost all kinds that are to do,
Blacksmithing, Tinkering, mason work,
When could I find a time to shirk?
Clock work, Jenny work, keeping school
Enough to puzzle any fool.
An endless list of chores and notions,
To keep me in perpetual motion.

Most if not all of Isaac's clocks were wall pieces. The date was painted in black on the face, and on the back of the dial a serial number, the name and date, and a bit of verse. Recorded clocks with the numbers 18, 21 and 22 (see Plates 16 and 42) suggest a considerable output, and probably many of the eighty-five pieces in use at the first family in 1858 may be ascribed to this craftsman. The dimensions of these three clocks are identical (roughly, 31 inches x 10 inches x 3 inches), and the common date, "May 12th, 1840," indicates "mass" or concurrent production. The frames are finished, top and bottom, with a plain quarter-round molding. In clocks No. 18 and 22, the bottom door is simply paneled in pine, the remainder of the frame being walnut. The door of clock No. 21 has glass panels separated by a medial cross-strip of wood. A hole in a crested extension of the backboard allowed the clock to be hung on a peg or nail. The twenty-four hour, "straight-line" movements are weight-driven, with verge escapement. In the absence of a backplate, the rear bushings were set directly into the backboard of the case. The escape wheel, bushings and suspension spring are brass; the pivots are steel; the hands and the minute and hour wheels are thin, hammered iron; but the other wheels and pinions are wood. The cord holding the weight runs over a pulley wheel projecting from the top of the case. A chrome yellow wash was applied to the interiors and the surface was varnished.

A philosophical time sense marks the verses inserted on the reverse side of the dial:

O let each one his moments well improve
To gain abiding bliss in realms above.
                              [*Clock No. 18*]
O Time! how swift that solemn day rolls on
When from these mortal scenes we shall be
   gone!!.   [*Clock No. 21*]
O swiftly see! each moment flies!
See and learn, be timely wise
Seize the moments as they fly,
Learn to live and know to die. [*Clock No. 22*]

The face of a wag-on-the-wall type of clock (Plate 4) is white-enameled, numbered and dotted in the same precise man-

ner as the pieces just mentioned. The hands are filed into the same shape, and the movement is almost identical, even to the shape of the small bone click and click spring. The dial is pine rather than hammered iron, and an arabic "1" on the back suggests it may have been Isaac's first clock, made at New Lebanon in 1815.* The wire staple for hanging and the wooden casing enclosing the movement and protecting it from dust, indicate that it was never intended to be used as part of a tall-clock.

Isaac Youngs's own record of his work is so symbolical of the experimental techniques of all Shaker craftsmen and mechanics, that we have been tempted to quote in full his CLOCK MAKER'S JOURNAL *with Remarks & Observations. Experiments etc. Beginning in* 1815.†

NARRATIVE

WHEN I was a child, I lived with my uncle, who was a clock maker—I used to be with him in his shop & watch his motions, learned the parts of a clock, & could put one together perhaps when 6 or 7 years old, & knew the time of day before I could talk plain. I had a relish for clocks & liked to be among them & to handle the tools, but as I left my uncle, the spring before I was 10 years old, I did not arrive to much understanding or judgment in the business. I went where no such thing was carried on & clocks were scarce. I however retained some notion about them, & wanted to make one with a knife awl etc. but I had poor convenience for it—sometime after I began it, my brother, Benjamin found it out & meeting me once said, "*Well, Isaac, how do you come on with your clock.*" I was a little confounded, but wishing to express in short my difficulties I replied "*Do you think I can make a clock go with a wooden wafer?*"

I dropped the matter & did no more about making clocks till the spring before I was 22.

*The clock in Plate 4 conforms to the style of items No. 12 and No. 13 in Isaac's Journal.
†MS. in collection of the Western Reserve Historical Society. (Courtesy of Wallace H. Cathcart.)

In these days I was pretty closely bound to tayloring, but occasionally did more or less choars—I got in to have some privilege in the shop with Amos Jewett who had made wooden clocks, he was very clever to me. I got liberty and went on to make a little timepiece for the elders' shop. I had a good many things to fix, made a tooth engine to go in the lathe, on a cheap scale.

And undertook a new manner of making the wheels, ie. to have wood cogs set in pewter rims, in that respect I succeed pretty well, they look a little finer style than wood wheels, but I had a good deal of difficulty to make my work true—my pivots were very course & pinions not very true & it was some time before I could make it runn well. I however succeeded so that with a very heavy weight it would go. I learned a good deal by this, found in particular that large pivots make a clock go hard in proportion,—also that the pinions had better be too small than too large.

This little rough production of my first fair attempts I called No. 1. After this I occasionally made timepieces & kept improving my knowledge, tools & conveniences, so that after making several I could make tolerable good ones. I have repaired the timepieces, & since the first start made 16 new ones, making some experiments by the way, as the follow statements will show.

ISAAC N. YOUNGS.

New Lebanon.
March 28th 1835.

JOURNAL

MARCH 24 1815. Finished a little time piece, for the use of the elders shop, & it being the first I have made of course it must be called No. 1.

Remark.—The first bob that I put to this seemed to be too heavy, I put a light-bob to it & the piece went much better—from which I inferred that a clock may sometimes go well with a lighter bob, when it would not with a heavy one.

October 1816. 19. Finished a cheap kind of timepiece, having made it in about 32 hours. No. 2. No case, but some little sort of doors, each side of the plates to enclose the wheels.

November 1816. From 25th to 30th. Made two timepieces, No. 3 & No. 4. To have cases.

Put on to these faces a last coat of copal varnish, but I find it to be a poor way, it turns yellow etc.

January 1818. 10. Finished an alarm timepiece. No. 5. For the east house, with a good cherry case.

October 1818. & November 1818. Finished an alarm timepiece No. 6. for the West house—with a cherry case.

Also made a common timepiece No. 6. with a case for the Blacksmiths.

July 1820. 4th Finished a striking clock. No. 8. I began it in May 1819 & worked at it by little at a time & I reckoned it took me about 40 days to make the clock & case. I put in iron boxes for the pivot holes, thinking this might perhaps do better than brass.

July 6, 1821. I find that the *iron* boxes a very poor thing for pivots to run in, for they cut away the pivot very fast. I therefore try bushing the pivot hole with silver.

October 21, 1821. Finished a little timepiece. No. 9. For the use of the elder sisters, in their work shop. The crown wheel of this is placed on the back side of the back plate & the palate has no shaft, but only operates on a short pin—for winding up, the key passes thro' the face. One brass pinion, the rest english box.

Pivots of steel knitting needles save the first & last wheels—I like the construction of it very well.

August 1822. 17th About finished a rough cheap timepiece No. 10. Made with one pointer, to go round once in 6 hours & having 2 rows of figures on the face or dial. Without a case.

October 1822. 1st. Finished a cheap timepiece, in form like the above. No. 11. For the Brethren at North Enfield [N. H.], taken home by Marshall Dyer & Otis?

February 1830. 13. Finished two timepieces, Nᵒˢ 12 & 13. No. 12 I put in the washhouse, & No. 13 in the new machine shop. These were a plain style with tin front plates, pivotholes boxed with brass or silver. Wheels of cherry—the pillars screwed into the back board which forms the back plates. Made to hang on a pin, with no case but a boxing round the wheels.

October 1831. Made some experiments to prevent chafing on the foot of the hammer staff, where the pins raise the hammer. By putting on a facing of silver: burnished the pins & let them run without oil, & I find after several months running that it does exceeding well, whereas formerly the bare iron coming in contact, it would run but a few weeks. Silver in such a case I believe is an excellent thing to prevent chafing by friction.

November 1832. 29th. Finished two time-pieces. No's. 14 & 15. Chiefly made along with the two last mentioned, in the same style. One I put in the Deaconesses shop & the other, [15] in the physician sisters' shop.

March 1835. 26th. Finished a timepiece. No. 16. Different plan from any I have made—it has no pillars—is set in the case & has only one plate, easily taken out—I like the manner very well.

.   .   .   .   .

I meant to have written some useful remarks in this book from experiments. But alass time flies & I am no more in time!

ISAAC N. YOUNGS.

& so reader *you* must follow me.

The equipment of Isaac's shop in the third story of the brethren's shop (erected in 1826) illustrates how eighteenth-century traditions of craftsmanship were prolonged by the Shakers far into the next century. In a period when factory production had almost completely supplanted hand work, when commercial clocks could be cheaply obtained, the Shakers preferred to be independent and to exalt the early manual methods. The foot lathe, the anvil (set on a wooden block with tools conveniently placed in encircling iron bands), the small forge and bellows, the Shaker-made tools, the superb workbench occupying one end of the room under the windows—these appurtenances were symbols of the principle that hands were the essential factor in all worthy achievement.

Another Shaker clockmaker who may also have been inspired by, and possibly apprenticed to Benjamin Youngs, was Cal-

vin Wells (1772–1853), a member of "the noble, royal Wells family" of fourteen, all but one of whom joined the Watervliet community soon after its organization. Calvin was the son of Thomas and Abigail (Youngs) Wells, and a younger brother of Seth Youngs Wells, one of the finest scholars in the United Society. On his mother's side he was therefore related to the famous clockmaking family, and the single product of his industry recorded bears (except for the simplicity of the dial numbers) a close resemblance to the Western Reserve item mentioned above. The Wells clock (in the collection of Mrs. John C. Spring of West Gloucester, Massachusetts) also has simple moldings at the top and base of the hood, as well as at a junction in the case just below the long, narrow door. The hood measures $11\frac{1}{2}$ inches wide by 7 inches deep; the upper section of the case, 10 inches by 6 inches. The height of the whole piece is 51 inches. On the back of the dial, which is seen through a round aperture in the hood, appears the inscription:

No. 3

CALVIN WELLS

MAKER 1817

Shaker clocks were also made in Canterbury, early in the last century, by Thomas Corbett, who organized the medicinal herb industry in that society, produced the famous Corbett's Compound Syrup of Sarsaparilla, and probably invented the electric batteries or static machines used by the Shakers in their medical departments. (See Plate 39.) On one of his clocks is the date "1810." The early shelf clocks from the Harvard community were sometimes made in mahogany, and would run eight days with two windings. At Sabbathday Lake a gong clock was used to summon the workers from the fields. Invented by Granville Merrill sometime after the Civil War, it is noteworthy for having the face on the inside of the building, and only the gong and bell on the outside.

C

Notes on construction, materials and finishes

THE CONSTRUCTION OF DRAWERS.

The drawer, considered as a unit and apart from its environing case, was as useful, ubiquitous, and as emblematical of order as the pegboard. The one or two wooden pulls with which each was provided are reminiscent of seventeenth-century cabinetwork. (Plate 44.) The shafts are threaded or driven in, and sometimes pinned on the inside. The knobs were usually made of maple or cherry, though rosewood appears occasionally on Niskeyuna furniture. Small brass pulls were also used at Hancock, Watervliet and other places. The presence of such commercial accessories as white china, Rockingham, mahogany or decorative wooden handles indicates late manufacture.

The drawer fronts on much early furniture, especially that produced in Maine, were fastened to the sides with a shouldered corner or nailed rabbet joint; but the standard practice was to secure the joining with lap dovetailing. In desk-boxes and small cabinetwork, the pins are small and most delicately wrought, and the dovetails themselves relatively large. The flush-bottom drawer is rare, this part being usually fitted into grooves cut in the front and back-boards. The sides, end and bottom of most drawers were pine, but maple, whitewood, chestnut and butternut were also used.

The cross-strips or rails between the drawers were attached to the sides of the frame by housed joints, shouldered on one or both sides. Except in occasional pieces where the drawers run into an enclosed box, the runners, guides or bearing-rails are rabbeted into the sides of the frame and nailed; a cross piece at the back adds support to the drawer when it is closed. In smaller pieces such as sewing cabinets, drop-leaf tables, stands and small counters, the framing around the drawers is secured by a stub mortise and tenon, further stiffened by glue and a dowel. The dust board was seldom absent from the base of the chest frame, and often was used between the drawers. In one piece, from the South family at New Lebanon, a hinged board between the two front feet prevents the accumulation of dust and dirt; it was to promote cleanliness, indeed, that chests and counters were often made to rest squarely on the floor.

MATERIALS.

In New Lebanon as well as in other eastern societies, white or soft pine was the most commonly used furniture wood. Almost every society owned extensive tracts of woodland, rich in coniferous growth; and "clear stuf" timber, readily adaptable to cabinetwork, was both accessible and inexpensive in the early years of Shakerism. Pine was the universal material for cases of drawers, cupboards, chests, wood-boxes, counters, benches, washstands and numerous other items. Black cherry, yellow birch, basswood, beech, butternut and maple were likewise employed. Rock or sugar maple was common in table and stand legs, bed-posts, chair posts, stiles and any parts requiring strength; sometimes a piece (candlestand, small chest or table, etc.) is made entirely of hard maple.

Soft or swamp maple and native walnut were also utilized, sometimes for counter tops or kitchen, bake-room and pantry pieces. Curly, or less often bird's-eye, maple was frequent in all types of craftsmanship: chair-posts and slats, stool seats and legs, table tops and legs, counters, desks, cases of drawers, measuring-sticks, chopping bowls, oval boxes, mirror frames and small tools. Ash was used for sieve rims and certain coopers-ware, ash or hickory for the rockers, rungs and sometimes the slats of chairs. White oak, chestnut, elm, hemlock and spruce are occasionally found in parts of pieces. Pearwood was not unknown, and journals reveal the "rough turning" of apple-tree timber for certain uses. Black walnut was used in the Groveland and western societies, and employed on rare occasions in the east for making wall-clocks. Mahogany was imported on few occasions, and then for some exceptional function.

With the passage of time, timber shortage was acutely felt in certain families. Scarcity of lumber was said to have been the main reason for the removal of an early society at Gorham, Maine, to New Gloucester. At the New Lebanon Church, maple "logs" and "clear stuf" pine or cherry were constantly being bought early in the last century. In 1805, for instance, the deacons purchased four ash trees for three pounds, one white oak tree for twelve shillings, and one pine tree for two shillings, sixteen pence. A maple log cost eight shillings in 1807, one dollar and a quarter in 1818, and two dollars in 1834. In the 1820's and 1830's, when building construction and furniture making were at their height, pine, cherry, whitewood and other kinds of lumber were purchased in quantity, often from other families or societies.

A distinctive feature in much Shaker pine furniture is the disclosure of the edge-grain of the wood, achieved by quarter-sawing or radially cutting the timber. The effect of fine transverse grain lines on the varnished or stained sides and drawer fronts of high cases is delightful. This method of cutting the logs was supposed to render the material harder and less liable to check or warp than plain-sawed timber. Wide boards were common in the early furniture. The backboards on low and high chests, cases of drawers and cupboards, and the boards used for the tops of counters and tables, sometimes measure from two to nearly three feet in width.

FINISHES.

It is commonly supposed that the Shakers disliked color as well as ornament. So subdued and quiet was the sectarian taste that outsiders, accustomed to bright hues or color "effects," were often insensitive to the low-keyed charm of Shaker decoration, and reported the color sense of the Believers as drab or non-existent. The leaders of the sect, however, were apparently more interested in regulating the nature of pigments, paints and dyes, and in making them uniform, than in suppressing a natural instinct. Thus, in one community, "window curtains must be white or of a blue or green shade but not checked nor striped." "Carpets of wool warp must not exceed three colors, black, green and red. . . . Filling to be course tow colored brown." "Carpets made of rags are not to exceed two colors." The interior woodwork of meeting-houses was to be painted blue, the floors of dwelling-houses a "reddish yellow," shop floors a "yellowish red." And so on.

That the Believers were not severely restrained in their effort to make fabrics modestly attractive is likewise attested by early weave-shop records on dyeing. In one account (from Watervliet), directions were given for dyeing cotton a madder red, catechu brown, fancy blue, London brown, copperas, orange, yellow, green and slate. Wool was dyed black, orange, fancy blue, yellow, green, scarlet, lavender, madder red or drab; and silk could be colored orange, slate, brown, red, crimson, blue, green, black or purple.

Color was freely employed in other industries. Herb labels and seed envelopes were printed in attractive yellows, greens, blues, oranges and lavenders. Dry extracts were put up in bright green cylindrical boxes of cardboard. Spools and spool stands were tinted red. A mottled or yellow finish was often applied to bookbindings and the leaf edges colored in blues, greens or yellow chromes. Boxes were finished in many colors.

In obtaining red dyes, madder was often combined with cream of tartar and alum, or with alum and sour bran soaked in sour beer. Logwood, camwood, red tartar, "Nicwood," redwood, and cochineal were also used. "A catechue color" was derived from blue vitriol, bichromate of potash and catechu. "Orange on cotton" was obtained from bichromate of potash and sugar of lead. Green was made from fustic combined with logwood and blue vitriol, or from copperas and logwood. Yellows were procured from fustic, from sugar of lead and bichromate of potash, and also from saffron, barberry bush, peach leaves or onion skins. Common birch bark, "stripped from the trees in autumn," made "a very beautiful nankin dye." Hemlock bark, butternut bark and sumac were used for brown. Blue was obtained from vitriol (often combined with copperas and prussiate of pot-

ash), from garden "pussly" and logwood, or from Prussian blue and oxalic acid. Winter pantaloons, in the early days, were dyed a reddish brown or claret color, summer vests a light blue. The winter dress of "females" was a wine-colored alpaca, drugget or worsted. Stocks were of blue silk, and Sabbath neckerchiefs of silk in various colors. A characteristic Shaker cloth was woven of bright red cotton and blue worsted.

Color was no less sparingly used in finishing furniture. Various oils, varnishes and light umber or sienna water paints or stains gave chairs, stands and other pieces a cinnamon, russet or tawny brown hue. Red was commonly applied to shop furnishings, and originally to meeting-house benches, counters, cupboards, chests and wood-boxes. Tables, sewing stands, candlestands, school-desks and chairs were at times painted the same color, though the shade varied, and the common term, "Shaker red," is not an exact designation. Old lift-top chests may be an ochre-red, later ones a terra-cotta. A washstand in the authors' possession is a light coral red. A color like Pompeian red or "dragon's blood" was used in the shops; and a kind of Chinese red was applied to the banisters, the paneled entrance door and even the floors of the old nurse-shop at Enfield (New Hampshire), built in 1795. A distinctive and delightful "reddish-yellow" or orange was possibly as common as the true reds. A floor rack for a trunk is an apricot-orange, while other pieces have a reddish-yellow tone which escapes orange but is not readily definable. Yellow paints and stains obtained from chrome or ochre were occasionally used on chairs, sinks and case-furniture, but more often on oval boxes, spit-boxes and other kinds of coopers-ware. The shade, however, is no more uniform than the reds, varying from a pale lemon-yellow to canary or to the yellowish-red used on the floors of shops; "Shaker yellow" is also a misnomer. The green paint on early "bedsteads" and on furniture or other objects used by the ministry was almost a bottle-green. The same color is occasionally found on chairs and oval boxes, but was not otherwise popular. Blue was more common, especially in meeting-house woodwork and furnishings. The interiors of certain cupboards and the surface of at least one large blanket-chest from Maine are a sky-blue color. A sewing desk from Sabbathday Lake is painted a pale blue. The pegboards, casings and the built-in drawers of meeting-houses may vary from a greenish to a Prussian blue. Paint of a robin's-egg blue was used on the woodwork and even the floors of certain chambers at Alfred. Turquoise and other blues were common on the interior of Enfield (New Hampshire) built-in cupboards. Various shades were used on oval boxes.

The first furniture made in the society was usually given a preservative coat of paint, but soon the custom prevailed of thinning the paint or using stain, often so light that the natural wood was visible. Water stains were obtained by mixing water with dry color, boiling and rubbing on. A smooth surface was effected by the final use of pumice stone and wax. A Watervliet "common-place book"* gives a number of interesting receipts, from which the following are extracted:

Red stain for wood, leather, papers.

Take 1½ oz. Brazeil dust, put it in 1 pt. of Alcohol—warm it a little in a water Bath, or on a Stove—say ½ hour, then put in, say, about

*Receipt Book Concerning Paints, Stains, Cements, Dyes, Inks, Etc. Rosetta Hendrickson. A present from Eld. Austin. MS. Watervliet, n.d. (c. 1849).

One teaspoon full of Bookbinder's acid, which will turn it to a beautiful red. The above will also make RED INK, only use good strong vinegar instead of Alcohol, and Purple INK, by using Logwood. The ink will need a little gum arabic.

Lacker.

Take 1 Gall. Linseed Oil
1 lb. Literage [litharge?]
¾ lb. Red Lead, ground fine. Boil slowly until it is so thick, it will not strike thro writing paper, which will take the most of a day to accomplish. Stir it often, and add when partly cool One Gall. Spts. Turpentine, and bottle for use.

White with blue shade.

To 100 lbs. White Lead or Zink, add 1 oz. Prusian Blue and 1 oz. Lampblack. Take the Lead and stir in Black and Blue, until you get the shade you desire.

Sky Blue for New Meetinghouse Chh. Watervliet 1849. Inside work.

To 10 lbs. White Lead, put 1 lb. Prussian Blue, mixed in Linseed Oil and drying Materials. For the meeting room doors etc. a little Varnish was added.

The Shaker account books reveal frequent purchases of red lead, which was mixed with oil and turpentine. Spanish white, Spanish brown, white lead, black lead and "spruce yellow" were also bought in quantity. The two following formulas, for blue and red, are taken from an early Hancock manuscript:

To Color blue on wood.

Pulverize 1 oz. best spanish Float Indigo, put it into 7 ozs. Sulphuric Acid in a glass vessel—let it stand 2 days. When used put a quantity sufficient into pure water and add Pearlast till the shade suits.

To Color Pink or Red on Wood.

Put one lb. of chipped Nicaraqua Wood to 1 Gal. pure water, boil 10 minutes in a brass vessel; then brush or dip the article in it and after brush it over with the following mixture, viz. to 1 oz. Muriatic acid add 1 oz. Grained Tin, leave out the stopper of the bottle till the Tin is dissolved. When the wood is dry—varnish.

In 1845 the Millennial Laws decreed that

Varnish if used in dwelling houses, may be applied only to the moveables therein, as the following: viz. Tables, stands, bureaus, cases of drawers, writing desks or boxes, drawer faces, chests, chairs, etc. etc.

It was also allowable on "banisters or hand rails" and on carriages "kept exclusively for riding or nice use."

During the second quarter of the century varnish was increasingly employed by the Shakers, popularized perhaps by the home manufacture of copal and "japan" brands, and approved for the protective surface it afforded. In the interests of uniformity, economy or tradition, however, the laws expressly forbade the use of varnish on "ceilings, casings, or mouldings," and on such objects as oval or "nice boxes." Much of the furniture produced in the two decades before the Civil War had a thin finish of varnish colored with the customary stains.

BIBLIOGRAPHY

THE sources listed below include: (1) expositions of the doctrines and religious culture of the Shakers, written in most cases by leaders of the society; and (2) references bearing more or less directly on the Believers' craftsmanship. Since practically no work has been done on the folk art of this sect, it seemed important to record, as far as possible, such minor allusions to furniture and Shaker artisanship as existed in scattered publications.

The best public collections of Shaker literature are in the Berkshire Athenæum (Pittsfield, Massachusetts), the Library of Congress, the library of the American Antiquarian Society, the Grosvenor Public Library (Buffalo, New York), the Connecticut State Library at Hartford, the New York City Public Library, the New York State Library at Albany, the Ohio State Archaeological and Historical Society at Columbus, the Western Reserve Historical Society (Cleveland, Ohio), Williams College Library and the Wisconsin Historical Society. A private library of books, manuscripts, prints and industrial records is owned by the authors.

I. DOCTRINE AND CULTURE

Authorized rules of the Shaker community. Mount Lebanon, N.Y., 1894. 16 pp.

AVERY, GILES B. Autobiography by Elder Giles B. Avery, of Mount Lebanon, N.Y. Also an account of the funeral service which was held at Watervliet, N.Y., December 30, 1890; together with testimonials of respect from his many kind friends. East Canterbury, N.H., 1891.

BAKER, ARTHUR. Shakers and Shakerism. In: New Moral Series. Edited by Arthur Baker, M. A. No. 2. London, 1896. 30 pp.

[BISHOP, RUFUS (Comp.). Revised by Seth Y. Wells.] Testimonies of the life, character, revelations and doctrines of our ever blessed mother Ann Lee, and the elders with her; through whom the word of eternal life was opened in this day of Christ's Second Appearing: collected from living witnesses. By order of the ministry, in union with the church. Hancock, 1816. 405 pp.

BROWN, THOMAS. An Account of the People called Shakers; their faith, doctrines, and practice, exemplified in the life, conversations, and experience of the author during the time he belonged to the society. To which is affixed a history of their rise and progress to the present day. Troy, 1812. 372 pp.

—— Columbia County at the End of the Century. A Historical Record of its Formation and Settlement, its Resources, its Institutions, its Industries and its People. In two volumes. Hudson, 1900. 748 pp. & 132 pp. & 440 pp. (Chap. XXXI, Vol. II, The Town of New Lebanon, includes an account of the Shakers by A. G. Hollister.)

CONRAD, JOSEPH. The Mirror of the Sea. New York, 1906.

DIXON, WILLIAM HEPWORTH. New America. Third edition. Philadelphia, 1869. 495 pp. (Chapters 42–46 relate to Mount Lebanon Shakers.)

DWIGHT, TIMOTHY. Travels; in New-England and New-York. In four volumes. New-Haven, 1822. (Vol. III, pp. 149–169, contains an account of Dr. Dwight's visit at the New Lebanon community in 1799.)

ELKINS, HERVEY. Fifteen years in the senior order of Shakers; a narration of facts concerning that singular people. Hanover, 1853. 136 pp.

EVANS, FREDERIC WILLIAM. Autobiography of a Shaker, and revelation of the Apocalypse. Mount Lebanon, N.Y., 1869. 162 pp.

FERGUSON, C. W. The confusion of tongues. A review of modernisms. New York, 1928. (Chapter 15: Shakerism.)

[GREEN, CALVIN and WELLS, SETH Y.] A summary view of the Millennial Church, or United Society of Believers (commonly called Shakers). Comprising the rise, progress and practical order of the Society; together with the general principles of their faith and testimony. Published by order of the ministry, in union with the church. Albany, 1823. 320 pp.

HARRIS, A. B. Among the Shakers. In: *The Granite Monthly*. Vol. I, No. 1. April, 1877. Dover, N.H., pp. 21–24.

HASKETT, WILLIAM J. Shakerism unmasked, or the history of the Shakers; including a form politic of their government as councils, orders, gifts, with an exposition of the five orders of Shakerism, and Ann Lee's grand foundation vision, in sealed pages. Pittsfield, 1828. 300 pp.

HINDS, WILLIAM ALFRED. American Communities. Oneida, N.Y., 1878. 176 pp.

—— American Communities. Chicago, 1902. (Revised edition.) 433 pp.

HOWELLS, W. D. Three Villages. Boston, 1884. 198 pp.

——A Shaker Village. In the *Atlantic Monthly*. Vol. XXXVII. No. CCXIX. June, 1876.

LAMSON, DAVID R. Two years' experience among the Shakers: being a description of the manners and customs of that people, the nature and policy of their government, their marvellous intercourse with the spiritual world, the object and uses of confession, their inquisition, in short a condensed view of Shakerism as it is. West Boylston, 1848. 212 pp.

MACE, AURELIA G. The Aletheia: Spirit of Truth. A series of letters in which the principles of the United Society known as Shakers are set forth and illustrated. Farmington, Me., 1899. 135 pp.

MACKAIL, J. W. The Life of William Morris. London, 1899. In two volumes.

MacLean, J. P. A sketch of the life and labors of Richard McNemar. Franklin, Ohio, 1905. 67 pp.

Manuscripts. Covenant of the Church of Christ, in New Lebanon, relating to the possession and use of a Joint Interest. 1795.

—— Covenant or Constitution of the Church of the United Society in the town of New Lebanon. n.d. 1830?

—— Millennial Laws, or Gospel Statutes and Ordinances adapted to the day of Christ's Second Appearing. Given and established in the church for the protection thereof by Father Joseph Meacham and Mother Lucy Wright, the presiding ministry, and by their successors the ministry and elders. Recorded at New Lebanon Augst 17th. 1821. Revised and re-established by the ministry and elders Octr. 1845.

—— Orders Rules and Counsels for the People of God, Written by Father Joseph to the Elders of the Church at New Lebanon. Copyed agreeable to Father Joseph's Word. February 18, 1841. 66 pp. (Bound with copy of Millennial Laws.)

—— Stewart, Philemon. Holy Laws of Zion. New Lebanon, N.Y. May, 1840.

[Meacham, Joseph.] A Concise Statement of the Principles of the Only True Church, According to the Gospel of the Present Appearance of Christ. As held to and practised upon by the true followers of the Living Saviour, at New Lebanon, Etc. Together with a letter from James Whittaker, Minister of the Gospel in this day of Christ's second appearing—to his natural relations in England. Dated October 9th, 1785. Printed at Bennington, Vt., by Haswell & Russell, 1790. 24 pp.

Nordhoff, Charles. The Communistic Societies of the United States. New York, 1875. 439 pp. (pp. 117–258 contain an account of the Shaker societies.)

Noyes, John Humphrey. History of American Socialisms. Philadelphia, 1870. 678 pp. (Chapter 45 relates to the Shakers.)

Pelham, R. W. A Shaker's Answer to the Oft-Repeated Question, "What Would Become of the World If All Should Become Shakers?" Boston, 1874.

Pomeroy, M. M. (Mark Mills). Visit to the Shakers. (At Canterbury Shaker Village, N.H.) n.d. 1899?

Robinson, Charles Edson. A concise history of The United Society of Believers called Shakers. East Canterbury, 1893. 134 pp.

Shaker Periodicals.
The Shaker. Vol. I, Jan. 1871, to Vol. II, Dec. 1872. Shakers, N.Y.
Shaker and Shakeress. Vol. III, Jan. 1873, to Vol. V, Dec. 1875. Mt. Lebanon, N.Y.
The Shaker. Vol. VI, Jan., 1876, to Dec., 1876. Shakers, N.Y., and Shaker Village, N.H.
The Shaker. Vol. VII, Jan., 1877, to Dec., 1877. Shaker Village, N.H.
The Shaker Manifesto. Vol. VIII, Jan., 1878, to Vol. XI, Dec., 1881. Shakers, N.Y.
Shaker Manifesto. Vol. XII, Jan., 1882, to Vol. XIII, Dec. 1883. Shaker Village, N.H.
The Manifesto. Vol. XIV, Jan., 1884, to Vol. XXIX, Dec., 1899. Shaker Village, N.H.
(Shaker Village, N.H., refers to Canterbury or East Canterbury; Shakers, N.Y., to Niskeyuna or Watervliet.)

Warder, W. S. A Brief Sketch of the Religious Society of People called Shakers. Communicated to Mr. Owen by Mr. W. S. Warder of Philadelphia, one of the Society of

Friends. London, 1818. (Early description of "beautiful workmanship" on Hancock meeting-house, and of the use of color in interiors.)

WICKLIFFE, ROBERT. The Shakers. Speech of Robert Wickliffe. In the Senate of Kentucky—Jan. 1831. On a bill to repeal an act of the General Assembly of the State of Kentucky, entitled, "an act to regulate civil proceedings against certain communities having property in common." Frankfort, Ky., 1832. 32 pp.

WHITE, ANNA and TAYLOR, LEILA S. Shakerism. Its meaning and message. Embracing an historical account, statement of belief and spiritual experience of the church from its rise to the present day. Columbus, Ohio, 1905. 417 pp.

[YOUNGS, BENJAMIN S.; DARROW, DAVID; MEACHAM, JOHN.] The Testimony of Christ's Second Appearing. Containing A General Statement of All Things Pertaining to the Faith and Practice of The Church of God in this Latter-Day. Published in Union. By Order of the Ministry. Lebanon, State of Ohio: From the Press of John M'Clean. Office of the Western Star. 1808. 600 pp.

—— —— Albany, 1810. 620 pp.

II. FURNITURE AND CRAFTSMANSHIP

ANDREWS, EDWARD D. and FAITH. Craftsmanship of an American Religious Sect. Notes on Shaker furniture. In the magazine *Antiques*, Vol. XIV. No. 2. August, 1928. pp. 132–136.

—— The Furniture of an American Religious Sect. In the magazine *Antiques*, Vol. XV, No. 4. April, 1929. pp. 292–296.

—— An Interpretation of Shaker Furniture. In the magazine *Antiques*, Vol. XXIII, No. 1. January, 1933. pp. 6–9. (See also camera studies of ministry's dining room and family dining hall. With short text. In *Antiques*, Vol. XXII, No. 6. December, 1932, p. 232.)

ANDREWS, EDWARD D. The Community Industries of the Shakers. New York State Museum Handbook 15. Albany, 1933. 322 pp.

—— The New York Shakers and their Industries. New York State Museum (Albany, N.Y.) Circular 2. 8 pp. October, 1930. (Illustrations of furniture and industrial objects.)

—— The Furnishings of Shaker Dwellings and Shops. (Descriptive catalogue for exhibition of furniture, industrial material and textiles of the Shakers of New England and New York. Berkshire Museum, Pittsfield, Mass. October, 1932.)

—— Shaker Furniture. Interpretative essay issued at time of exhibit of Shaker furniture at Lenox, Massachusetts, August 23 to September 8, 1934. Lenox Library Association. (Folder.)

—— Shaker Handicrafts. Introduction to catalogue of exhibit of Shaker furniture and inspirational drawings at the Whitney Museum of American Art, New York, November 12 to December 12, 1935. 15 pp.

BRIDGES, MADELINE S. A Wonderful Little World of People. In the *Ladies' Home Journal*, June, 1898. (Illustrations of late interiors at Mount Lebanon.)

CATALOGUES OF CHAIRS. Illustrated catalogue of Shaker chairs, foot benches, floor mats, etc. Mt. Lebanon, Columbia County, N.Y. Albany, 1874. 29 pp.

—— Centennial Illustrated Catalogue and Price List of the Shakers' Chairs, Foot Benches, Floor Mats, etc., Manufactured and sold by the Shakers at Mt. Lebanon, Columbia Co., N.Y. Also containing several pieces of Shaker music. Albany, 1876.

—— Illustrated catalogue and price list of Shakers' chairs, manufactured by the Society of Shakers. R. M. Wagan & Co., Mount Lebanon, N.Y. Pittsfield. n.d. 16 pp.

—— —— Canaan. n.d. 18 pp.

CORNELIUS, CHARLES OVER. Early American Furniture. New York, 1926. (Reference on p. 251 to Shaker chairs.)

DYER, WALTER A. The Furniture of the Shakers. A Plea for its Preservation as Part of our National Inheritance. In *House Beautiful*, Vol. LXV, No. 5. May, 1929.

DYER, WALTER A. and FRASER, ESTHER STEVENS. The Rocking-Chair. An American Institution. New York, 1928. (Brief treatment of Shaker chairs, pp. 36–41.)

HOOPES, PENROSE R. Connecticut Clockmakers of the Eighteenth Century. New York, 1930.

KETTELL, RUSSELL HAWES. The Pine Furniture of Early New England. Garden City, New York, 1929. (Plates 81 and 118.)

KEYES, HOMER EATON. Article in the magazine *Antiques*. New York, October, 1934.

KOEHLER, ARTHUR. The Identification of Furniture Woods. Miscellaneous Circular No. 66. United States Department of Agriculture. Washington, D.C. November, 1926.

MANUSCRIPTS. Account books and trustees' records of the Church, or Church family, at New Lebanon. 1787–1865.

—— Journal of Henry DeWitt.

—— Discharge papers of the New Lebanon Church.

—— Indenture agreements between elders of New Lebanon Church and various individuals.

—— Miscellaneous trade papers, letters, circulars, architects' plans, etc.

—— New Lebanon Ministry Sisters Journal.

—— Youngs, Isaac N. Clockmaker's Journal with Remarks & Observations. Experiments etc. Beginning in 1815.

—— Youngs, Isaac Newton . . . His History in Verse. July 4, 1837.

O'BRIEN, HARRIET E. Lost Utopias. A brief description of three quests for happiness, Alcott's Fruitlands, Old Shaker House, and American Indian Museum. Rescued from oblivion, recorded and preserved by Clara Endicott Sears on Prospect Hill in the old township of Harvard, Massachusetts. Boston, 1929. 62 pp. (Pictures of interiors of a small Shaker dwelling.)

Report of the Commissioner of Patents for the year 1852. Washington, 1853. (Brief description [p. 423] of ball-and-socket device for Shaker chairs.)

Report of the trustees of the United Society of Shakers in the town of New Lebanon, Columbia Co., N.Y. State of New-York. No. 89, In Senate, Mar. 19, 1850. 14 pp.

SHACKLETON, ROBERT and ELIZABETH. The Quest of the Colonial. New York, 1921. (Mention of Shaker chair, with cuts.)

STOREY, WALTER RENDELL. Native Art from Old Shaker Colonies. A Distinct Style of American Furniture which has Interest for our Times. In the *New York Times Magazine*, October 23, 1932. (Sisters' retiring-room illustrated.)

TAYLOR, HENRY HAMMOND. Knowing, Collecting and Restoring Early American Furniture. Philadelphia, 1930.

WHITE, A. J. The 100th Anniversary of the founding of a Community. Almanac for 1888, issued by A. J. White, 54 Warren St., New York. (Line cuts of herb and schoolrooms, showing chairs and desks.)

WINGATE, CHARLES F. Shaker sanitation. Broadside. (Reprint from *The Sanitary Engineer*. New York. September, 1880.)

YOUNGS, SELAH. Youngs Family. Vicar Christopher Yonges. His Ancestors in England and His Descendants in America. A History and Genealogy. New York, 1907. 377 pp.

INDEX